FOREWORD

Winter, spring, summer or fall...
each time of the year is special in its
own unique way. This book helps
you celebrate the seasons by making
your own creations using soft and
versatile fleece.

You'll find clear instructions, helpful
fleece facts, patterns and diagrams
to guide you on your way to a
successful project.

Turn the page and embark on a
journey through the seasons.

TABLE OF CONTENTS

WINTER

SPRING

SUMMER

AUTUMN

FLEECE FACTS

Please familiarize yourself with the following facts and information before beginning the projects in this book.

Fleece is usually 60" wide. It's important to cut off the selvage edges before measuring the fleece for your project.

To determine the right and wrong side of the fleece, stretch the fabric along the cut edge of the fleece. The fleece will curl to the wrong side. Mark your cut piece with a marking pencil before you start your project.

Fusing: For adding appliques to projects, we've found that Steam-A-Seam2® works well. It can be used for both adding appliques and joining two pieces of fabric together. It's available in various widths, from hemming tape to packaged sheets or by the yard.

When using any fusing products, always follow the manufacturer's instructions before beginning.

Tracing the patterns: Place tracing paper over the pattern and trace the pattern. Cut out the pattern along drawn lines. Pin the pattern to the fleece and cut out.

Marking fleece: A Chacopel pencil is great for marking. It's available in either light or dark chalk so that it can be used on any color of fleece. After marking, you can use the brush on the end of the pencil to erase your marks.

Fabric care: Fleece doesn't shrink, so there's no need for pre-washing.

For laundering, use a powdered laundry detergent and luke warm water on a gentle cycle. Liquid fabric softeners shouldn't be used.

For drying, place in the dryer with no dryer sheets and dry on low for a short time.

For ironing, use steam and a pressing cloth. Never touch the iron directly to the fleece.

Hemming edges or lining fleece is optional. This depends on your own personal preference.

Curling fringe: Some fleece fabrics curl really well and others don't. Before you purchase your fleece, test a small piece. Your fabric store clerk will let you try a small sample. Cut a strip ½" wide across the crosswise grain, then stretch it and see if and how much it will curl.

To curl the fleece for your finished project, hold onto one end of the fringe and pull the other end tightly. See page 92 for an example of curled fringe.

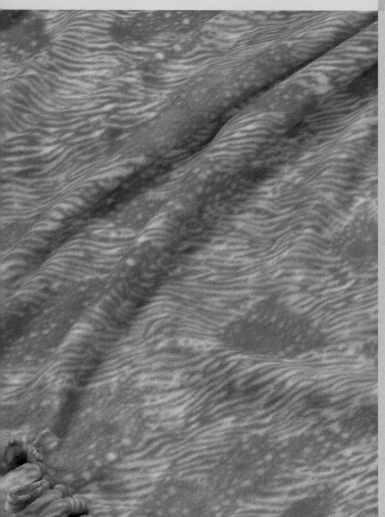

General supplies needed:

Measuring tape
Fabric marker
Pins
Iron
Pencil
Yard stick
Chacopel pencil
Tracing paper
Pressing cloth
Scissors or rotary cutter
Pinking shears

> Note:
> It's helpful to have a small, sharp scissors for accurately cutting appliqués.

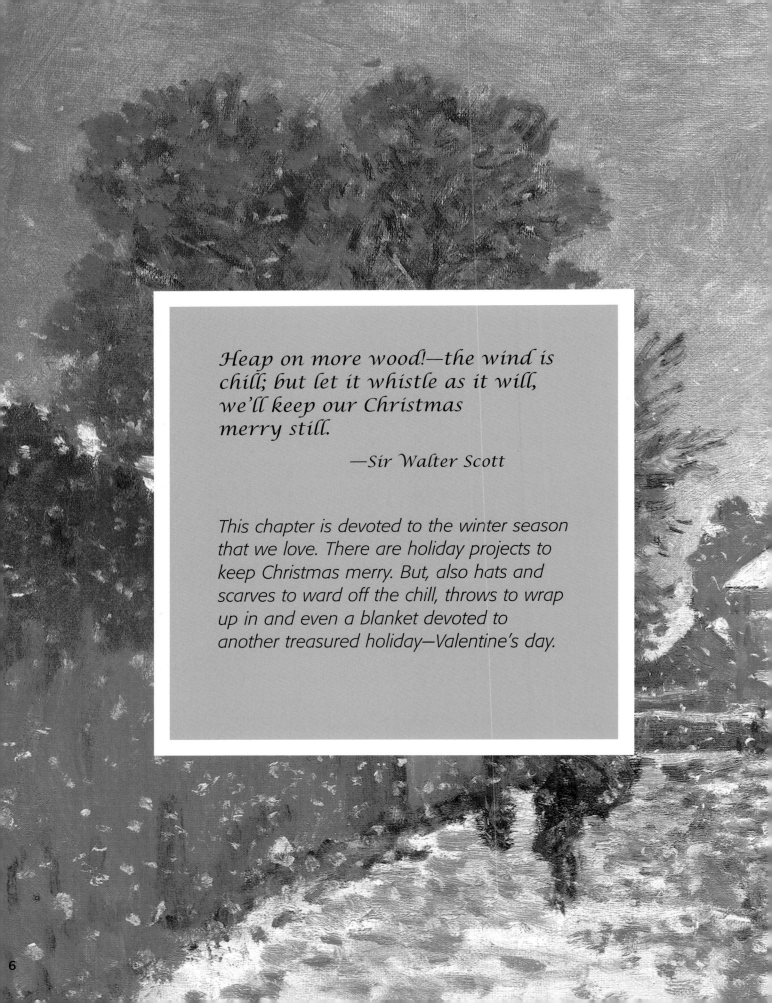

Heap on more wood!—the wind is chill; but let it whistle as it will, we'll keep our Christmas merry still.

—Sir Walter Scott

This chapter is devoted to the winter season that we love. There are holiday projects to keep Christmas merry. But, also hats and scarves to ward off the chill, throws to wrap up in and even a blanket devoted to another treasured holiday—Valentine's day.

WINTER

BRIGHT AND MERRY

Colors brighten up the holidays, particularly when they are as imaginative as these. Bright pink, turquoise, lime green and purple may not seem traditional. But when combined with other Christmas decorations in the same shades, you've got a winning combination. This quilt is bordered with cheerful ball fringe and decorated with typical Christmas images.

You'll need:
Fleece:
  ¼ yd. bright pink
  ¼ yd. purple
  ¼ yd. turquoise
  1½ yds. lime green
4 yds. lime green ball fringe
Steam-A-Seam2® fusible web

Finished size: 27" x 33½"

1. To make the quilt, cut the fleece as follows: five 7½" squares each of lime green, turquoise, purple and pink. Cut one piece of green fleece 27" x 33½".

2. To form the quilt top, sew the squares together using a ½" seam allowance. Refer to the photo at right for square placement.

3. Pin the ball fringe to the quilt back along the edges and sew in place.

4. Place the large piece of green fleece on a flat surface. With wrong sides together and edges matching, pin the quilt top to the green fleece.

5. Topstitch the quilt top to the green background piece along all four sides.

6. To add appliqués: Trace the Christmas shapes (patterns on page 111) onto one side of the Steam-A-Seam. Cut around the images. Peel off one side of the backing paper and place the adhesive side onto the appropriate square of fleece. Cut out the shapes.

7. Place the shapes on the appropriate squares of the quilt (referring to the photo). Peel off the backing paper and place a pressing cloth over the top of the cut-out. Iron onto the square. Repeat for all the shapes.

This grouping of unique stockings will dress up your holiday. From the comic snowman, to the sharp triangle of a tree, to the vibrant polka dots, these stockings will delight Santa. They're edged with ball fringe and appliquéd with blanket stitching for real holiday pizzazz.

COOL CHRISTMAS STOCKINGS

Snowman

You'll need:
Fleece:
  ½ yd. lime green
  Scrap of white, pink, purple
  and orange
Embroidery floss: black, white,
  purple, and bright pink
12" white ball fringe
Craft glue

Christmas Tree

You'll need:
Fleece:
  ½ yd. bright pink
  ¼ yd. lime green
  Scraps of yellow, turquoise,
  lavender
12" lavender ball fringe
Embroidery floss: turquoise, lime
  green, yellow, and bright pink
Craft glue

Polka Dots

You'll need:
Fleece:
  ½ yd. turquoise
  Scraps of yellow, purple,
  lime green, red, bright pink
Embroidery floss: purple,
  lime green, red, and bright pink
12" lime green ball fringe
Craft glue

1. Use the pattern on page 109 to cut out the stockings and the patterns on page 110 for the appliqué pieces.

2. For the snowman: Use three strands of black floss and French knots to add eyes and mouth to the small round head piece of the snowman and "buttons" to the other body pieces (refer to photo for placement). Glue the orange nose to the face.

3. Sew the snowman body pieces to one stocking piece using three strands of white floss and a blanket stitch.

4. Sew the hat to the snowman's head using three strands of purple floss and a blanket stitch.

5. For the scarf: Cut purple fleece ½" x 9". Fringe each end of the scarf and tie in a knot. Glue or tack to the neck of the snowman.

6. Sew the small white polka dots around the snowman (refer to photo) using three strands of white embroidery floss and a blanket stitch.

7. For the other stockings: Stitch the pieces to the stockings using three strands of floss and a blanket stitch. Vary the color of the floss or refer to the photograph for color placement.

8. For all three stockings: Place the two stocking pieces wrong sides together and sew using three strands of floss and a blanket stitch.

9. Glue the ball fringe around the top edge of the stocking.

10. For the hanger: Cut a ¾" x 6" strip of matching fleece. Fold in half and glue or stitch in the top corner of the stocking.

Blanket stitch instructions:

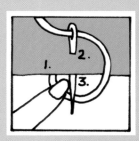

1. Come up at 1. Go down at 2 and come up at 3, keeping floss below point of needle. Continue stitching, keeping stitches even.

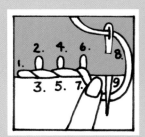

ON THE DOT

This tree skirt delights and surprises and is sure to make the season bright and merry. The shocking pink skirt is merrily decorated with big vibrant dots of color. Alternating shades of embroidery floss blanket stitch the dots to the skirt...a double layer of ball fringe gayly embellishes the edges.

You'll need:
Fleece:
   1¼ yds. bright pink
   Scraps of turquoise, yellow, orange, lime green and purple
Ball fringe: 3½ yds. each lime green and purple
Craft glue (optional)

1. Fold a 60" square of the pink fleece into fourths.

2. To make a pattern: Cut a square of paper the same size as the folded fabric (30" x 30"). Take a piece of string (approximately 35") and tie one end around a pushpin and the other end around a pencil. The distance between the pin and pencil should equal the radius of the tree skirt (30"). Put the pin at corner A of the paper holding the pencil at right angles; draw an arc from B to C.

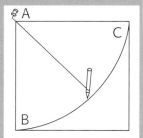

3. Repeat step 2 to mark the inner cutting line for the center opening. The distance between the pin and pencil should be 3".

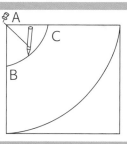

4. Pin the pattern to the folded fabric and cut through all layers of fleece.

5. For the opening at the back of the skirt, cut through one layer of fleece along one fold from the outer edge to the inner circle.

6. Trace the circle pattern (page 110). Pin to the various colors of fleece and cut out to make approximately 15 polka dots. Pin the polka dots randomly to the skirt. Using alternating colors of embroidery floss and a blanket stitch, sew the polka dots to the skirt.

7. Sew or glue the ball fringe around the edge of the skirt, first the purple, then the lime green (see photo).

HOMESPUN FLEECE

Here's an alternative version of a tree skirt to deck your home with gladness. Perfect for a country farmhouse or a rustic cabin, this holiday accessory is not only attractive, but can be created in less than an hour. The fleece is available as a panel with the fringe printed right on. All you have to do is cut the fringe and make an opening for the tree and Voila! One holiday decoration out of the way!

You'll need:
Fleece:
  Patchwork panel

This fabric is sold by the panel. For this tree skirt, you'll need one panel.

Finished size: 47" x 58"

1. To make the tree skirt, fold the fabric in fourths. Pin the circle pattern (page 22) on the corner of the fold and cut the hole.

2. Cut a slit on one side of the fabric from the edge to the hole.

3. Cut ¼" x 3" fringe all the way around the edge.

> **Tip:**
>
> The instructions above can also be used to make a no-sew poncho. Use steps 1 & 3 only. Look for other printed fleece panels that would work for tree skirts or ponchos.

SANTA AND HIS FRIENDS

Designed by Holly Witt Allen

Santa Ornament

You'll need:
Fleece:
  White
  Red
  Flesh
Polyester fiberfill
Embroidery floss: black, white
  and red
½" pom poms: one each
  red and white
Craft glue

1. Use the patterns on page 108 to cut out the Santa pieces.

2. Glue the beard to one head piece. Stitch the eyes using three strands of black embroidery floss and French knots.

3. Place head pieces right sides together. Using a ¼" seam allowance and leaving the bottom edge open for turning, sew the pieces together, making sure not to catch the bottom of the beard in the stitching. Clip curve and turn right side out. Stuff with fiberfill and sew the opening closed.

4. Glue the mustache and the red pom pom to the face. Make several vertical cuts in the beard to create fringe. Curl the fringe by holding one end of a strip and pulling the other end.

5. Glue hat around the top of the head, overlapping long edges. Glue on the hat brim, overlapping ends at the back. Glue the white pom pom to the point of the hat. Fold down the point of the hat and glue.

6. For the hanger: knot ends of a 7" length of red floss together. Sew the knot to the back of the Santa.

Reindeer Ornament

You'll need:
Fleece:
  Brown
  Beige
  Green
Polyester fiberfill
Embroidery floss: black and red
Two ½" red pom poms
Two small twigs for antlers
Craft glue

1. Use the patterns on page 108 to cut out the reindeer pieces.

2. Glue the muzzle to one head piece. Stitch the mouth using three strands of black floss and a straight stitch, and the eyes using French knots.

3. Place head pieces right sides together. Using a ¼" seam allowance and leaving an opening for turning at bottom, sew pieces together. Clip curves and turn right side out. Stuff with fiberfill and sew the opening closed.

4. Glue inner ears to outer ears.

5. Make small openings in the seam for the antlers and ears. Glue antlers and ears into openings.

6. For the hanger: knot ends of a 7" length of red floss together. Sew the knot to the back of the reindeer.

7. Glue on the red pom pom nose and holly berry and green holly leaf to the top of the head.

Snowman Ornament

You'll need:
Fleece:
  White
  Black
  Plaid
  Green
  Orange
½" red pom pom
Embroidery floss: red and black
Polyester fiberfill

1. Use the patterns on page 108 to cut out the Snowman pieces. Cut one ½" x 9" plaid with pinking shears for the scarf.

2. On one head piece, stitch the eyes and mouth using three strands of black floss and French knots.

3. Place head pieces right sides together. Using a ¼" seam allowance and leaving an opening for turning, sew the pieces together. Clip curves and turn right side out. Stuff with fiberfill and sew the opening closed.

4. Knot the scarf around the bottom edge of the head; glue.

5. Roll nose into a cone and glue the sides together. Glue the nose to the head.

6. Use black floss to sew a running stitch along the gathering line on the hat. Pull the ends to gather the hat to fit the head; knot ends. Glue hat to head.

7. Glue the leaf and pom pom to the hat brim.

8. For the hanger: knot ends of a 7" length of black floss together. Sew the knot to the back of the Snowman.

How about creating a little holiday merriment? These cute ornaments are sure to delight the kids and your guests as well. They'll definitely add gaiety to your yuletide festivities. These handcrafted trimmings can decorate a tree or become favors for your holiday table.

17

TABLE TRADITION

You'll need:
Fleece:
  ½ yd. royal blue
  ⅛ yd. gold
Steam-A-Seam2® hemming tape

Hanukkah is such an important holiday. An attractive table runner for the menorah will certainly add to the occasion. This lovely accessory is fashioned of traditional blue and gold. The gold strips are woven through the blue fleece to lend style to the Hanukkah festivities.

1. Cut the blue fleece 15" x 20". Cut 1" slits in the fleece every inch, starting 2½" from the long edge and 3" from the short edge (as shown in the diagram).

2. Cut the gold fleece into two 1½" x 11" strips and two 1½" x 17" strips.

3. Weave the 11" strips through the slits on the short ends of the runner. Pin to secure. Weave the 17" strips through the slits on the long ends. Pin. Weaving should start and end on the back of the runner.

4. Cut squares of hemming tape and apply to the ends of each strip. With a pressing cloth over the top, iron the strips on the back of the runner to secure.

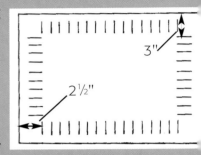

FESTIVAL OF LIGHTS

Candles burning in a menorah are a special Hanukkah tradition. Jewish families light candles in the menorah to celebrate the miracle of the burning lamp and religious freedom. This banner commemorates that miracle. Nine candles are appliquéd to the banner beautifully signifying this ancient and sacred story.

You'll need:
Fleece:
   ³/₄ yd. royal blue
   ¹/₈ yd. gold
   ¹/₈ yd. white
   ¹/₈ yd. rust
2 yds. gold cord, ½" wide
2 gold tassels
1" dowel, 26" long

1. Cut blue fleece 24" x 24".

2. Use the patterns on page 110 to cut the candles and flames. Pin the candle patterns on white fleece and cut out nine pieces (eight small and one large). Pin the flame pattern on gold fleece and also cut out nine pieces. Cut out a strip of the rust fleece 1½" x 21".

3. Turn one side of the blue fleece under 2" and sew along the raw edge to form a casing. This becomes the top of the banner.

4. Position and pin the rust strip to the bottom of the banner. Pin the candles on the banner in a playful manner (refer to photo). Sew the strip and candles to the banner using a zigzag stitch.

5. Position flames on the banner and glue or hand stitch.

6. Thread the dowel through the casing. Tie the cording on the ends of the dowel and glue on the tassels.

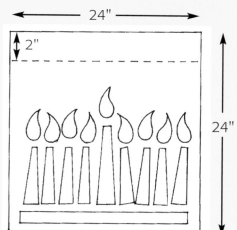

A WARMING TREND

Winter becomes you. Especially when you're wrapped up in warm and toasty fleece. This dashing duo is tailor-made with the merriest red plaid and bright green and red solids. The scarf is trimmed with fashionable fringe, and the stylish hat is topped with a "button" of green fleece.

Red Plaid Scarf

You'll need:
Fleece:
  ½ yd. red plaid
  ⅛ yd. red
  ⅛ yd. green

1. Cut the red plaid fleece 8" x 58".

2. Cut two pieces of the red fleece and two of the green 4½" x 8".

3. Place the red fleece ½" up from the edge on the short end of the scarf. Topstitch ⅛" along the top edge of the red fleece. Do the same with the other piece of red fleece on the other end of the scarf.

4. Sew the green fleece 1" above the red following the sewing instructions in step 3. Topstitch again ⅛" from the first stitching.

5. Cut ½" x 3" fringe on the green fleece and ½" x 4" fringe on the red fleece.

Red Plaid Hat

You'll need:
Fleece:
  ¼ yd. red plaid
  ½ yd. red
  Scrap of green

1. Trace the pattern for the hat crown on page 109. Pin the pattern on the red fleece and cut out four pieces.

2. Sew the crown pieces together using a ⅝" seam.

3. Cut the red plaid 8½" x 26½" to make the brim.

4. Sew the short ends of the brim together using a ⅝" seam. Fold the brim in half lengthwise with wrong sides together.

5. Sew the brim to the inside of the crown with raw edges and seams matching.

6. Sew another seam ¼" down from the first seam. Trim seam. Turn the hat inside out and turn up the brim.

7. For the "button", trace the pattern (page 110). Pin the pattern to a scrap of green fleece and cut out.

8. Use a running stitch to stitch around the circle ⅛" from the edge. Pull the thread tightly to gather.

9. Sew the "button" to the top of the hat.

SHALL WE SKATE

You'll need:
Fleece:
   1¼ yds. ice skate print
   4½ yds. white ball fringe

What better way to enjoy the winter season then cozied into this darling poncho? The printed fleece features colorful ice skates, and the poncho is trimmed all the way around with snowball fringe. She'll be the envy of the skating rink crowd when she makes her grand entrance in this tasteful topper.

1. Cut the fleece for the poncho 40" x 40". Fold in fourths (A). Place the pattern from the bottom of this page on the fold and cut out the hole for the neck (B).

2. Sew the ball fringe all around the edge of the finished poncho.

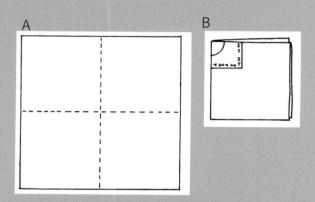

A   B

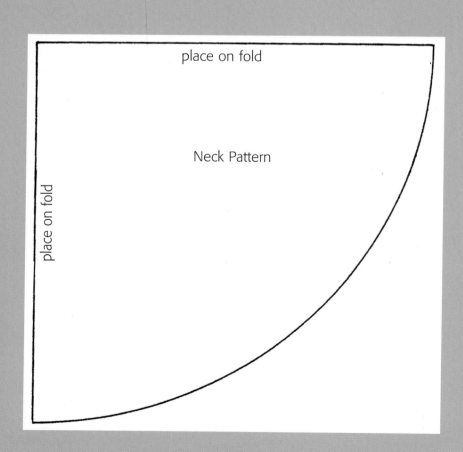

place on fold

Neck Pattern

place on fold

SKATING PARTY

When you wear this soft and comfy jacket, you'll have a real reason to welcome the cold. The patch pockets feature a pair of ice skates and that same print is echoed in the stylish scarf. Trimmed with strips of coordinating solids, it's ready to wrap around the pretty jacket.

You'll need:
Fleece:
  1½ yds. bright pink
  ¼ yd. lime green
  Squares of ice skate print
Embroidery floss: lime green and black

Fits child's size 4 - 7

1. Cut out the jacket following the diagram below.

2. Fold in half and sew the side seams using a ½" seam allowance.

3. Cut down the center front and round the corners slightly.

4. Cut two 6" x 6" lime green squares. Cut two 5" x 5" squares with the ice skate images.

5. Using six strands of lime green embroidery floss and a blanket stitch, sew the ice skate squares to the green squares.

6. Using six strands of black embroidery floss and a blanket stitch, attach the pockets to the jacket, sewing around the sides and bottom of each square (refer to the photograph for placement).

7. Blanket stitch around the edges of the jacket using six strands of lime green embroidery floss.

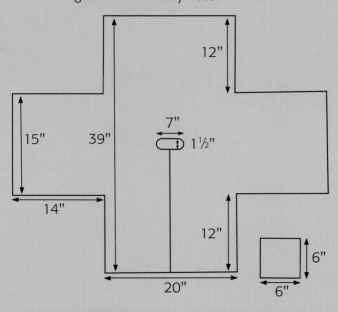

SKATER'S WALTZ

Here's the scarf again, this time paired with warm-as-toast mittens. Bright pink fleece is stitched together to form the mittens that are also embellished with the ice skate images. No matter how gusty the wind blows, you'll be warm as can be in this pretty pair.

Scarf

You'll need:
Fleece:
  ¼ yd. ice skate print
  Scraps of bright pink, turquoise and lime green

1. Cut the print fleece 8" x 59".

2. Cut two strips each of the bright pink, turquoise and lime green fleece ¾" x 8" using pinking shears.

3. Sew the three pinked strips on each end of the scarf starting 4" from the end and 1" apart. Refer to the photo for color placement.

4. Cut ¼" x 3" fringe on each short end of the scarf.

Mittens

You'll need:
Fleece:
  ¼ yd. bright pink
  Squares of ice skate print
Embroidery floss: lime green

1. To make a pattern for the mittens: Place your hand with fingers slightly spread on a piece of paper. Trace around it to make the pattern. You can use this same pattern for both hands just by reversing it.

2. Pin the pattern to two pieces of fleece for each hand. Cut out. Also cut out two 3" square ice skate images.

3. Sew the ice skate squares on one left and one right mitten piece using lime green embroidery floss and a blanket stitch (instructions page 11).

4. With the mittens right sides together, blanket stitch all around them using three strands of lime green floss.

FINE FEATHERED FRIEND

You can almost hear the cardinals singing on this delightful holiday throw. Consisting of solid panels stitched right down the middle and a print fleece square in the center, this winter-themed throw welcomes the season. The fancy fringed edges lend an easy, casual feeling to this warm and seasonal coverlet.

You'll need:
Fleece:
  ¾ yd. red
  ¾ yd. green
  1 yd. cardinal print (or any Christmas print)

Finished size: 42" x 56"

1. Cut the red and green fleece 21½" x 56".

2. Cut the print fleece 24" x 32".

3. Cut ¼" x 3" fringe on each short end of the print fleece. Tie the strips in knots (see photo).

4. Pin the red piece to the green piece and sew down the 56" length using a ½" seam allowance.

5. Center the print piece in the center of the throw. Topstitch this piece to the throw all the way around.

6. Cut ¼" x 3" fringe on the two short edges of the throw.

EMBOSSED ELEGANCE

You'll need:
Fleece:
  ½ yd. green
  ¼ yd. red
Foam stamps
Spray bottle of water
½ yd. gold tassel trim
Pressing cloth
Iron
12" pillow form

1. To emboss the fabric: Try the technique first on a small piece of fleece before beginning. A fuzzier fleece will emboss the best. Try each side of the fleece to see which side embosses better. Cut the green and red fleece a bit larger than the cut size you will need (see step 3).

2. Place the foam stamp (design-side up) on your ironing board. Place the fleece on top of the stamp. Place a pressing cloth on top of the fleece (A). Spritz the fabric with the spray bottle (B). Place your iron on top for a few seconds (C). Move the stamp or stamps from place to place and repeat the above procedure to emboss the pieces of fleece.

3. To make the pillow: Cut the green embossed fleece 13" x 24". Cut one piece of red embossed fleece 6½" x 12".

4. To form the flap: Center the red fleece on one short end of the green with right sides together and sew using a ½" seam allowance (A).

5. With right sides facing, fold the green fleece in half with the edges meeting just below the flap (B).

6. Sew the sides together using a ½" seam allowance. Turn right side out.

7. Sew trim along the bottom edge of the flap.

8. Insert the pillow form and fold the flap down.

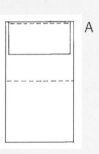
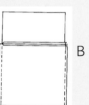

Can't find embossed fleece? Why not try making your own? It's easy. The embossing is done using foam stamps and an iron to make impressions in the fleece. What better way to start the holidays than creating your own Christmas accessories. The envelope pillow was made using the red and green embossed fleece. The gold tassel trim completes this elegant holiday treasure.

FROM THE HEART

Designed by Dana Whalen

For Valentine's Day and beyond, this romantic throw adorned with a million hearts celebrates the season. Draped casually over a bed, this symbolic coverlet adds a sentimental touch to the décor. Light the candles, turn on some soft music and turn a boudoir into a blissful sanctuary.

You'll need:
Fleece:
   2 yds. red with pink hearts
   2 yds. pink

Finished size: 56" x 66"

1. Cut both pieces of fleece 56" x 66".

2. Place the two pieces wrong sides together. Cut 1" x 3" fringe through both thicknesses.

3. To connect the two sides, tie the fringe all the way around the throw.

Hint:

This basic no-sew throw is an excellent project for beginners. It's so easy to make, even the kids can get involved. You'll be amazed at the wide variety of prints available and the huge array of solids at your local fabric store. Almost any combination of fabrics can be used to make a unique throw all your own.

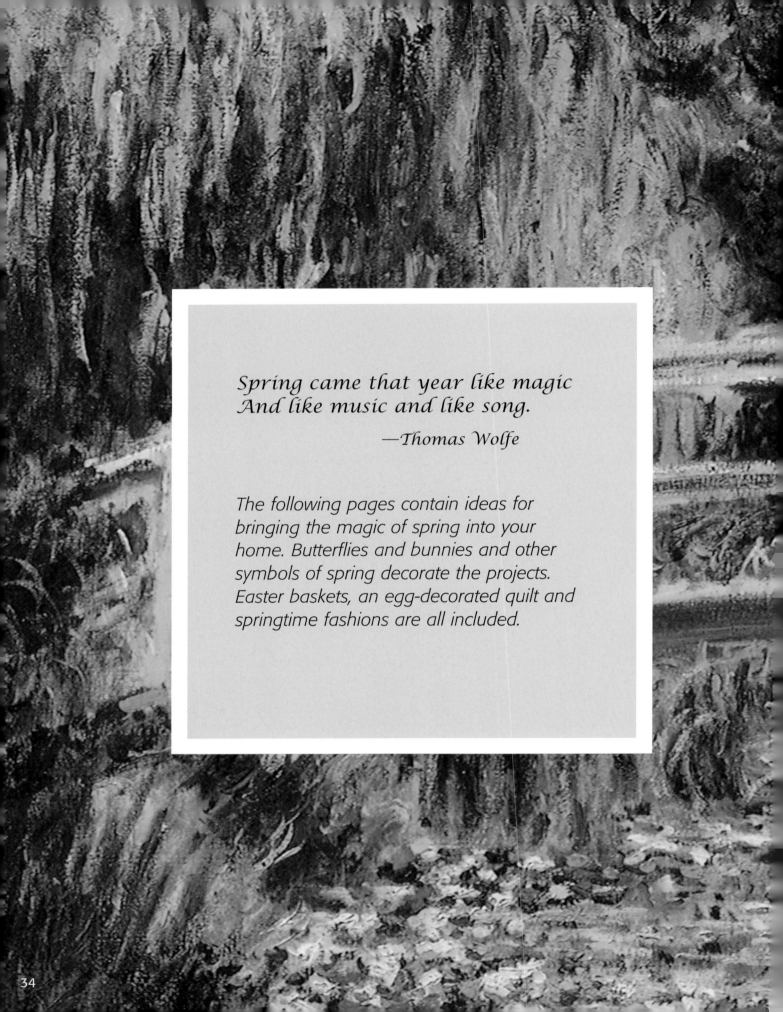

Spring came that year like magic
And like music and like song.

—Thomas Wolfe

The following pages contain ideas for bringing the magic of spring into your home. Butterflies and bunnies and other symbols of spring decorate the projects. Easter baskets, an egg-decorated quilt and springtime fashions are all included.

SPRING

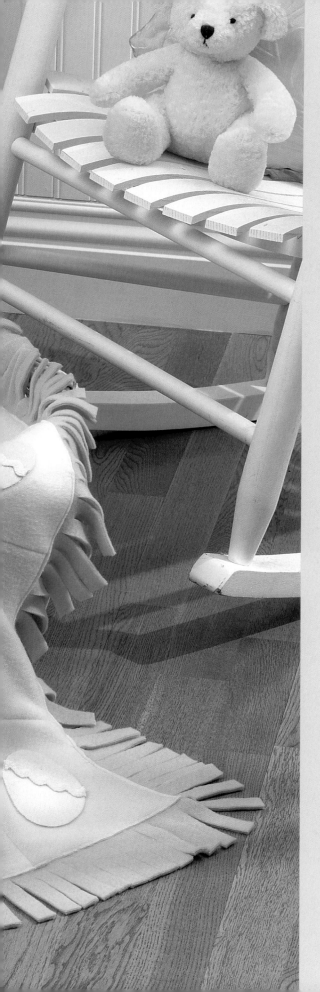

EGG HUNT

Pastel eggs parade across this delightful quilt, sure to dress up any child's room for the Easter season and beyond. Jumbo chenille rickrack decorates the eggs for an authentic rendition of dyed eggs. The lavender fringe completes this throw to perfection.

You'll need:
Fleece:
  1½ yds. lavender
  ¼ yd. green
  ¼ yd. pale yellow
  ¼ yd. pale pink
  ¼ yd. blue
  ¼ yd. rainbow print
Jumbo rickrack: 18" each of yellow, pink
  and lavender chenille
½ yd. Steam-A-Seam2® fusible web

Finished size 33" x 40"

1. For the eggs: Iron Steam-A-Seam to a piece of the rainbow fleece following manufacturer's instructions. Use the pattern on page 114 to trace ten egg shapes onto the paper side of the Steam-A-Seam. Cut out the egg shapes.

2. Cut rickrack to decorate eggs (refer to photo) and glue or hand stitch onto the eggs. Set aside.

3. Assemble the quilt: Cut fleece into 7½" squares as follows: three blue, four green, four yellow, four lavender and five pink.

4. Cut one piece of lavender fleece 33" x 40" for the backing.

5. To form the quilt top, sew the squares together using a ½" seam allowance. Refer to photo for color placement.

6. Place the lavender fleece on a flat surface. Center the quilt top on the lavender fleece and pin in place. There should be a 3" border around the quilt top.

7. Topstitch along all four edges.

8. Cut ½" x 3" fringe on all four sides of the border.

9. Peel off the backing paper from the eggs and position on the appropriate squares (see photo). With a pressing cloth over the top, iron the eggs onto the quilt.

BUNNY HOP

Round and round they go…leaping and frolicking on this charming pastel pillow. The bunnies, cut from soft white fleece seem to come alive as they jump from square to square. The pillow is edged with various shades of chenille rickrack to coordinate with the pastel patches.

You'll need:
Fleece:
  ½ yd. white
  ½ yd. green
  7" square pink
  7" square blue
  7" square lavender
Jumbo rickrack: 1 yd. each light blue and pink chenille
Embroidery floss: pink, blue, green, and lavender
12" pillow form

1. Cut out four white bunnies (pattern on page 113).

2. Cut 7" squares of pink, blue, green and lavender. Cut a 13" square of green for a backing piece.

3. Sew the bunnies to each square using a blanket stitch and three strands of embroidery floss (refer to photo for placement of bunnies on the squares). Alternate the colors of floss. Allow ½" on each side of the pillow for the seam allowance.

4. Sew all four squares together.

5. Cut each color of rickrack to fit around each fourth of the pillow. Sew rickrack to the edges of the pillow top alternating colors (see photo).

6. With right sides facing, sew the top and backing together on three sides using a ½" seam allowance.

7. Turn the pillow right side out. Insert the pillow form and hand stitch the opening closed.

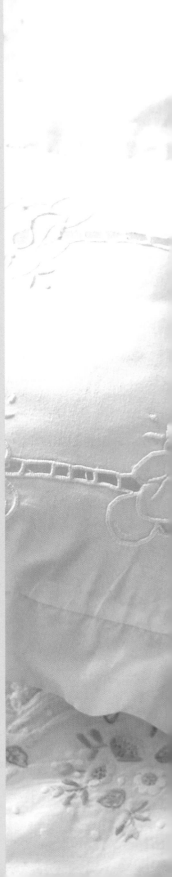

EASTER GATHERINGS

Kids, get ready. It's time for the annual Easter egg hunt. These charming baskets are empty now, but it's just a matter of time before they'll be full to the brim with the hidden treats. The baskets are dressed up in circles of soft pastel fleece and trimmed with a perky row of lavender fringe.

You'll need:
Fleece:
  Lavender
  Pink
  Yellow
Ball fringe: lavender
Craft glue

(The quantities of the fleece and ball fringe will depend upon the size of the baskets used.)

1. To make a pattern: Measure around the bottom of your baskets from point A to point B. Cut a square of paper the size of that measurement (C). Fold the paper into fourths and draw a curved line from D to E. Cut out the pattern, pin to the fabric and cut out.

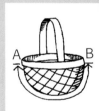

2. Sew a gathering stitch all around the edge of the circle. Place the basket on the center of the fabric and gather up to fit the top of the basket. Knot the thread.

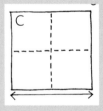

3. Glue the ball fringe all around the fabric, covering up the gathers.

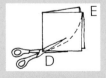

SPRING ROLL

We know it's spring when purple crocus crack through the ice, daffodils bloom and hydrangeas sprout in the garden. This fun roll pillow includes the shades of all those flowers. Three types of fleece are sewn together and then fringed for an easy and casual addition to the bed. The throw is simply fringed on the edges to complete this springtime picture.

Pillow

You'll need:

Fleece:
  ½ yd. yellow
  ½ yd. lavender
  ½ yd. pastel stripe
14" neckroll pillow form

Throw

You'll need:

Fleece:
  1½ yds. pastel stripe

Finished size: 48" x 60"

1. Cut the yellow fleece and the lavender fleece 13" x 21" and the striped fleece 12" x 21". Cut two strips of striped fleece ½" x 10" to use for the ties (step 8).

2. Fold the yellow fleece in half matching edges of short ends. Sew together using a ½" seam allowance starting in 3½" from one end and ending 2½" in from the opposite end.

3. Repeat step 2 with the lavender fleece.

4. Repeat step 2 with the striped fleece, but start sewing 2½" from one end and ending 2½" in from the opposite end.

5. Cut the fringe on the yellow and lavender fleece ½" x 3½" on one side and ½" x 2½" on the opposite side.

6. Cut ½" x 2½" fringe on both sides of the striped fleece.

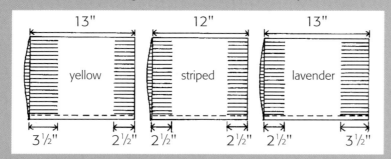

7. With the striped fleece in the center, tie the three sections together forming a tube.

8. Insert the pillow form in the tube. Gather the fringe at each end and tie with the ½" x 10" pieces of striped fleece.

9. For the throw: Cut the striped fleece 48" x 60". Fringe the edges of the throw ½" x 4".

Pretty as a picture. A spring-like plaid fleece is the fabric of choice for this super-simple, no-sew vest. It's bright and breezy enough to welcome spring. Wear with a simple white tee and pair it with the matching headband and you've got yourself the ideal outfit for an early morning stroll through the garden.

YOUNGER THAN SPRINGTIME

Vest

You'll need:
Fleece:
  1 yd. lavender-and-green plaid

Fits child's size 4-6

1. Follow the diagram to mark the measurements for the vest on the fleece.

2. Cut out the basic shape 20" x 32".

3. Cut up the center on the vest front.

4. Cut out the neckline and armhole area also following the diagram.

5. Fold the fabric in half with the short ends together and edges matching.

6. Cut 1" x 3" fringe on both sides following the diagram and tie the sides together.

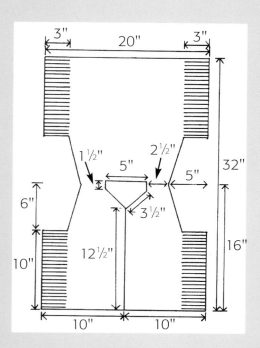

Headband

You'll need:
Fleece:
  Lime green

1. Cut a piece of lime green fleece 1" x 23".

2. At each short end, cut a 2" long slit.

3. Form a circle with the band and tie the two ends together.

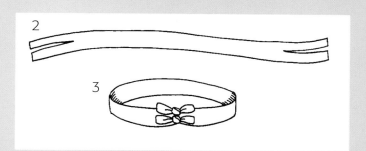

BUTTERFLY PARADE

Here's an Easter bonnet with lots of frills, and a matching purse as well. What little girl doesn't love butterflies? This dynamic duo sports butterflies as well as her favorite colors. How can you miss? The pink, blue and lavender shades of plush fleece combine to make this stylish set.

Butterfly Hat

You'll need:
Fleece:
 ⅛ yd. lavender
 ⅛ yd. pink
 ⅛ yd. periwinkle
 Scrap of green
Pink embroidery floss

1. To make the hat: Use the pattern (page 109) to cut out two each of pink, blue and periwinkle crown pieces.

2. Sew the six crown pieces together using a ¼" seam allowance.

3. Cut a piece of periwinkle fleece 3" x 22¼" for the brim.

4. Sew the short ends of the brim together using a ⅝" seam allowance. Fold the brim in half lengthwise with wrong sides together.

5. Sew the brim to the inside of the crown using a ⅝" seam allowance and with raw edges and seams matching.

6. Sew another seam ¼" down from the first seam. Trim seam. Turn the hat inside out and turn up the brim.

7. For butterfly appliqué: Use the patterns on page 112 to cut out the butterfly pieces.

8. Using a blanket stitch and three strands of pink floss, stitch the bottom wings (B) to the main piece (A). Then stitch the top wings (C) to piece (A). Stitch the body piece (D) down the middle of the wings. Tack the finished butterfly to the hat and brim.

9. For button: Trace the pattern for button on page 110. Using a running stitch, stitch around the circle ⅛" from the edge. Pull the thread tightly to gather. Sew the button to the top of the hat.

Butterfly Purse

You'll need:
Fleece:
 ⅛ yd. lavender
 ⅛ yd. pink
 ⅛ yd. periwinkle
 Scrap of green
20" jumbo rickrack: light blue chenille
Pink embroidery floss
Velcro® dots

1. Cut one 3" x 10" piece each of lavender, pink and periwinkle.

2. Sew the periwinkle and lavender pieces to the pink piece along the edge of the long side using ¼" seam allowance.

3. With right sides facing, turn the bottom edge up 4". Sew the sides together using ¼" seam allowance.

4. Turn the purse right side out. Trim the top edge to round the corners (refer to photo). This becomes the purse flap. Using three strands of embroidery floss, blanket stitch around the edge of the flap.

5. Position the ends of the rickrack inside the purse at the seams about ¼" from the edge. Turn each end under ¼". Sew in place.

6. For the butterfly appliqué: Use the pattern on page 112 to cut the butterfly pieces. Using a blanket stitch and three strands of pink floss, stitch the bottom wings (B) to the main piece (A). Then stitch the top wings (C) to piece (A). Stitch the body piece (D) down the middle of the wings.

7. Sew a piece of Velcro® to the bottom back of the butterfly and the opposite piece to the purse. Tack the top of the butterfly to the top flap of the purse aligning the Velcro® pieces (see photo).

SPRING FLING

The butterfly flutters from her fashions to her bedroom to add a touch of spring to the room's décor. This butterfly is appliquéd to the lavender pillow and bordered with a square of chenille rickrack for a soft, pastel texture.

You'll need:
Fleece:
  ½ yd. lavender
  ¼ yd. pink
  Scrap of periwinkle and green
1¼ yds. jumbo rickrack: light blue chenille
Embroidery floss: lime green and pink
Fabric glue
14" pillow form

1. Cut two 15" squares of lavender fleece. Cut one 7" square of pink fleece. Use the patterns on page 112 to cut the butterfly pieces.

2. Center the pink square on one lavender square and sew on using three strands of lime green floss and a blanket stitch.

3. Position the butterfly pieces on the pink square (refer to the photograph at left). Sew on using three strands of pink embroidery floss and a blanket stitch.

4. Sew or glue the rickrack around the pink square with 1" between the edges of the square and the rickrack.

5. With right sides together, sew the lavender squares together on three sides using ½" seam allowance.

6. Turn the pillow right side out. Insert the pillow form and hand stitch the opening closed.

Dress up her bed with a special-occasion pillowcase made just for her. Surprise her on Easter morning with this lovely lavender covering for her favorite pillow. A bevy of bunnies rings the case—each one cuter than the last. A simple band of pink rickrack completes the design.

You'll need:
Fleece:
  1 yd. bunny print
  ¼ yd. heart border print
2 yds. jumbo rickrack: pink chenille

1. Cut bunny fleece 25½" x 36½". Cut border print 5¾" x 36½".

2. Sew the top edge of the border print to the bottom edge of the bunny print using ¼" seam allowance.

3. With right sides facing, fold the assembled piece of fleece in half matching unfinished edges.

4. Sew around the top edge and the side edge using a ¼" seam allowance.

5. Turn the pillowcase right side out.

6. Turn the bottom edge of the border print under ½" and sew along the raw edge.

7. Measure up about 1" from finished edge and sew rickrack in place.

HERE'S MY HEART

A stream of pastel stripes runs diagonally across this heart-shaped pillow. The patterned fleece is plumped with polyfill to create a partner for the pillowcase at right. What a team!

You'll need:
Fleece:
  ½ yd. pastel print fabric
16" each jumbo rickrack: yellow, pink, and
  lime green chenille
Polyester fiberfill

1. Use the pattern on page 113 to cut out two heart pieces.

2. Position the rickrack on one heart piece (refer to photo for placement). Match the edge of rickrack to the edge of the pillow. Stitch or glue the rickrack across the heart.

3. Place both pieces of fleece right sides together, matching edges. Sew around the pillow using a ½" seam allowance. Leave a 3" opening to turn and stuff the pillow.

4. Turn the pillow right side out. Stuff with fiberfill and hand stitch the opening closed.

HIPPITY HOPPITY

Baby shouldn't be left out at Easter time. Here's a sweet gift to keep her smiling...a funny bunny made of plush fleece. The bunny's head is attached to a handle easy enough for a wee one to hold.

You'll need:
Fleece:
  ⅛ yd. white
  Scrap of pink
Polyester fiberfill
Embroidery floss: black

1. Use the patterns on page 112 to cut out ears, head and handle from the white fleece. Cut the inner ear and nose from the pink fleece.

2. Stitch the eyes using three strands of black floss and a satin stitch. Stitch the whiskers using a running stitch. Glue the nose to the face using craft glue. (As an option, the nose could be embroidered using pink floss and a satin stitch.)

3. Hand stitch the pink inner ears to the ears.

4. Pin ear fronts to backs and sew around the edges using a ¼" seam allowance leaving the bottom open. Turn right side out.

5. Pin the front of the head to the back, with right sides together, sandwiching ears where indicated on pattern and with edges matching.

6. Sew around the head using ¼" seam allowance, leaving an opening at the bottom. Turn right side out. Stuff with fiberfill.

7. Sew the front and back of the handle together leaving an opening at the end. Turn right side out. Stuff with fiberfill and hand stitch handle closed. Overlap the ends and slipstitch to the back.

Rich music breathes
In summer's every sound,
While o'er the mingling scenes
Far spreads the laughing sky.

—John Clare

Summertime seems made for lazy days—dining al fresco, sunning by the pool, catching fireflies, picnics on the grass and enjoying cool evenings on a porch. With the house garbed for summer, life shifts to the outdoors. Bright and colorful fleece projects are perfect to accompany these summertime activities.

SUMMER

SWIMMING LESSONS

You'll need
Fleece:
  1½ yds. bright yellow
  ¼ yd. gold
  ¼ yd. royal blue
  ¼ yd. turquoise blue

¼ yd. white
⅛ yd. orange
Ten tiny black buttons
Steam-A-Seam2® fusible web

Finished size: 33" x 40"

1. Cut ten yellow and ten white 8" squares. Cut one piece of yellow fleece 33" x 40".

2. To make the ducky squares: Trace the pattern pieces (page 119) on pieces of Steam-A-Seam (following the instructions on the patterns). Cut out the shapes and peel off the backing paper on one side. Apply the pieces to the appropriate fleece pieces and cut out. Peel off the other backing paper and position the fleece pieces on the quilt squares following the diagram.

3. With a pressing cloth over the top of the square, iron the pieces down. Check to see if all pieces are secure. If not, keep pressing until a proper bond is achieved. Repeat for all the decorated squares.

4. Sew the button eyes to the ducks as pictured.

5. For the quilt top: Sew the squares together using ½" seam allowance. (Refer to photo for color placement).

6. Lay the large piece of yellow fleece on a flat surface. Center the quilt top on the fleece. Pin and topstitch along all four edges.

7. Cut ½" x 2" fringe on all four sides of the yellow fleece.

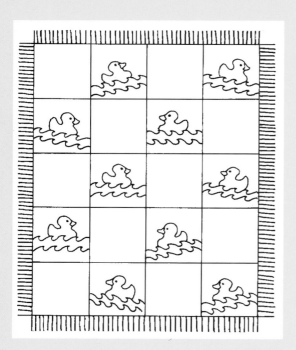

Note:
If using this throw for a baby or child under three, eliminate the buttons and use black French knots for the eyes.

Cheerful ducks swim in the choppy waves on this sunny and bright quilt. Either as a birthday gift for a child or a baby shower gift for a special friend, this quilt is sure to be a winner.

THREE'S COMPANY

Here's a shower gift certain to garner a roomful of "oohs" and "aahs"…a trio of fluffy blocks. Not only will these add to a baby's room décor, but also to a toy collection. When baby is ready to reach and play, these delightful blocks will be available for baby's attention. The blocks display animal images as well as alphabets to start baby on his or her way to creative learning.

Bunny

You'll need:
Fleece:
  ¼ yd. white
  ¼ yd. bright pink
  ¼ yd. turquoise
  Scrap of lime green
Steam-a-Seam2® fusible web
One ½" white pom pom
One tiny black button
Polyester fiberfill

Kitty

You'll need:
Fleece:
  ¼ yd. white
  ¼ yd. purple
  ¼ yd. turquoise
  Scrap of bright pink
  Scrap of gray
Steam-A-Seam2® fusible web
Two tiny black buttons
Black embroidery floss
Polyester fiberfill

Ducky

You'll need:
Fleece:
  ¼ yd. white
  ¼ yd. blue
  ¼ yd. turquoise
  Scrap of yellow
  Scrap of gold
  Scrap of orange
Steam-A-Seam2® fusible web
One tiny black button
Polyester fiberfill

1. For bunny block: Cut out six 6" squares: three white, two bright pink and one turquoise. Cut out one 3" lime green square.

2. For kitty block: cut out six 6" squares: three white, two purple and one turquoise.

3. For duck block: Cut out six 6" squares: three white, two blue and one turquoise.

4. For all three blocks: Trace the patterns (pages 116 & 117) on one side of the Steam-A-Seam. Cut around the shapes and peel off the backing paper on one side. Apply the pieces to the appropriate colors of fleece. Peel off the backing paper on the other side and position the shapes on one square of white fleece. Place a pressing cloth over the top of the square and iron the fleece pieces on.

5. For Bunny: Sew on the pink nose, white pom pom and black button.

6. For Kitty: Sew the eyes and nose to the face. Sew on the whiskers using black embroidery floss.

7. For Ducky: Iron on the beak. Sew the eye to the face.

8. For the alphabet square: Trace the appropriate letter and a 3" square (pink for kitty, green for bunny and gold for duck) onto Steam-a-Seam. Peel off the backing paper and apply the letter to the white fleece. Apply the 3" square of Steam-A-Seam on the back of the 3" square of the appropriate color of fleece. Cut out the letter. Peel off the other backing paper and place onto the colored square. With a pressing cloth on top, iron the letter onto the square. Iron this 3" colored square in the center of the 6" colored square.

9. Sew the block together: Pin the first square with the design along the top edge of the square with a ¼" seam allowance, and another square along the bottom edge, matching raw edges. Sew across both (A). Attach a fourth square along the bottom edges of the previous two squares and sew (B), making a complete square without the sides.

10. Pin another square around the top edges of the previously sewn pieces. Sew each side, stopping ¼" from each end and continuing onto the other sides in the same manner (C).

11. Sew the final square on, leaving a 3" opening on one side. Turn the block right side out and lightly stuff. Hand sew the opening closed.

Note:
If these projects are to be for a child under three, you might choose instead of using buttons, to embroider the eyes, tails and noses.

BRIGHT MEMORIES

Here's another baby shower gift idea…a small but delightful photo album decorated with a "B" for baby. Covered in a vintage-style chenille, the album is embellished with colorful squares of fleece, playful ball fringe and coordinating striped ribbon. All that's needed is the addition of some cute baby photos.

You'll need:
Small photo album, 5" x 7"
⅓ yd. white chenille fabric
Fleece:
  Scraps of pink, lime green and white
12" of ball fringe: lime green
28" pink-and-white striped ribbon, 1" wide
Craft glue

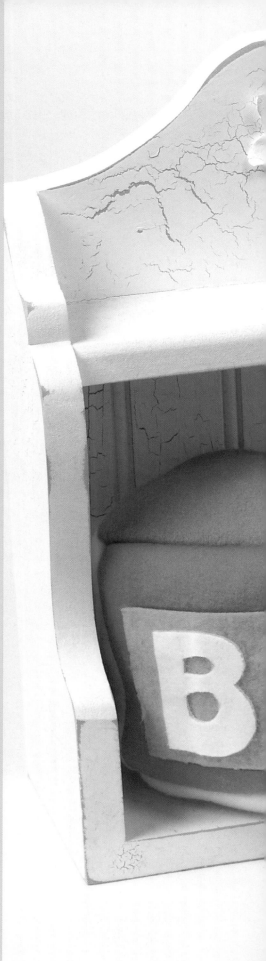

1. Cover the album by placing it opened on the wrong side of the chenille fabric. Trace around it with a pencil. Add 1" all the way around and cut out.

2. Lay the chenille wrong side up with the album on top. Apply a thin layer of glue to all corners and sides of the inside of the album covers. Pull the fabric up and into the glue. Trim as needed.

3. Cut the ribbon into two 14" lengths. Glue one to each inside cover. Cover the inside front and back with chenille or complementary fabric. Tie into a bow to close the album.

4. Trace the letter "B" for baby (page 116) on a small piece of Steam-A-Seam. Peel off one side of the backing paper and place the tracing on a square of white fleece. Cut out the "B" and set aside.

5. Cut a piece of lime green fleece 2¾" square and a pink piece 3¼" square.

6. Peel off the backing paper of the "B" and iron onto the center of the green square. Place a square of Steam-A-Seam on the back of the green square and iron to the center of the pink square.

7. Glue the length of ball fringe around the back edge of the pink square. Place a square of Steam-A-Seam on the back of the pink square. Peel off the backing paper and iron to the white album. Glue edges of the square to secure to the album.

STAND AND SALUTE

Hip hip hooray! Here's a trio of stars parading across a bed to show your patriotism. The red, white and blue fleece pillows are punctuated with buttons covered in stars and strips. What better way to pledge your allegiance?

You'll need:
Fleece:
   ²⁄₃ yd. blue
   ²⁄₃ yd. white
   ²⁄₃ yd. red
   ¹⁄₈ yd. print with stars & stripes
Six 1½" button forms
Polyester fiberfill
Heavy-duty thread or thin string
Upholstery needle

1. Use the pattern on page 114 to cut the six star pieces; two blue, two white and two red.

2. Pin the star pieces together and sew using a ½" seam allowance. Leave a 3" opening for stuffing. Trim seams and turn the stars right side out.

3. Stuff the pillows with fiberfill. Hand sew the opening closed.

4. Use the print fabric to cover the buttons (following the manufacturer's instructions).

5. Find the center of the front and back of the pillow and mark. Use a long length of the heavy duty thread or thin string and upholstery needle. Poke the needle through both the front and back at the marks. Leave a 4" tail on the back and pull the rest of the thread through. Thread one button onto the thread. Put the needle back through to the back (where the mark is). Take the 4" tail and the thread on the needle. Tie them together tightly. Tie one to two knots to secure. Slip the other button on the thread. Remove the needle. Tie the two pieces of thread together again tightly. Tie in knots under the button. Trim the thread.

FANTASY BOUTIQUE

Bring in da funk! Your daughter's room will be jazzed up with the addition of this totally cool throw. Colorful triangles border the center piece displaying funky purses, shoes and hats in a profusion of bright colors.

You'll need:

Fleece:
3/4 yd. red
3/4 yd. lime green
3/4 yd. bright pink

3/4 yd. gold
1 1/8 yds. print with shoes, hats and purses (or other novelty print)

1. Cut print fabric 36" x 36". Cut solid fabrics 25 1/2" x 25 1/2", then cut in half on the diagonal. You'll be using only half of each color. Save the other half for other projects such as the jumbo pillow on page 79.

2. Cut 1/4" x 3" fringe around the print fabric. Cut 1/4" x 3" fringe on the longest edge of each solid piece. Discard the triangle of fleece at each end of fringe.

3. Tie the fringe, connecting the solid pieces to the print piece.

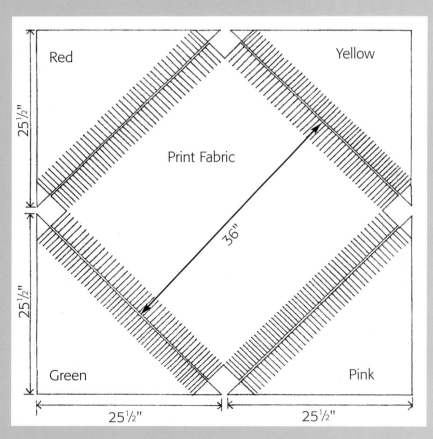

ACCESSORIZE, ACCESSORIZE

Shoe Pillow

You'll need:
Fleece:
  ⅔ yd. lime green
  ⅔ yd. pink
  ¼ yd. print with shoes, hats and purses
Steam-A-Seam2® hemming tape
Fabric glue
14" pillow form

1. Cut the pink and lime green fleece each into 21" x 22" pieces.

2. Cut a piece of the print fleece 7" x 7½" (with a shoe image).

3. Apply hemming tape around the edges of the back of the fleece with the shoe image. Peel off the backing paper of the tape and iron the shoe to the center of the lime green square.

4. Cut ¾" x 3½" fringe all around the edges of the lime green and pink pieces.

5. Tie the squares together using a double knot and leaving one end open. Insert the pillow form. Tie the fringe on the open end to close.

6. To make the pom pom for the shoe: Cut a piece of lime green fleece 1" x 10". Cut the fringe ⅛" x ¾". Gather this piece up in your fingers and glue together at the base. Glue the pom pom to the pillow.

Note:
When using an alternate print fabric, adjust the size of the pillow fronts according to the size of the image you'll be using.

Hat Pillow

You'll need:
Fleece:
  ⅓ yd. orange
  ⅔ yd. gold
  ¼ yd. print with shoes, hats and purses
1 yd. purple ball fringe
Steam-A-Seam2® hemming tape
Fabric glue
Polyester fiberfill

1. Cut two 19" circles of gold fleece (see page 12).

2. Cut one 9" circle of orange fleece and one 7" circle of the print fleece (with a hat image).

3. Apply the hemming tape around the edges of the back of hat image. Peel off the backing paper of the tape and using a pressing cloth, iron the hat image to the center of the orange circle.

4. Repeat step three adding the hemming tape on the orange circle and ironing to a piece of gold fleece.

5. Glue or sew the purple ball fringe around the orange circle.

6. Sew the gold circles together with right sides facing, using a ½" seam allowance. Leave a 3" opening for stuffing.

7. Turn the pillow right side out. Stuff the pillow with fiberfill and hand stitch the opening closed.

Purse Pillow

You'll need:
Fleece:
  ⅓ yd. pink
  ¼ yd. turquoise
  ¼ yd. print with shoes, hats and purses
1 yd. purple ball fringe
Steam-A-Seam2® hemming tape
Fabric glue
14" neckroll pillow form

1. Cut one piece of pink fleece 20" x 20" and two pieces ½" x 10" for the ties.

2. Cut one piece of turquoise fleece 7" x 9".

3. Cut one piece of print fleece 5¼" x 7¼" (with a purse image).

4. Apply the hemming tape around the edges on the back of the fleece with the purse image. Peel off the backing paper of the tape and apply to the center of the turquoise fleece. With a pressing cloth on top, iron the purse piece to the turquoise piece.

5. With right sides facing, sew the pink piece together on long sides using ½" seam allowance to form a tube. Turn right side out.

6. Repeat step 4 centering the turquoise fleece on the pink.

7. Glue or sew the purple ball fringe around the turquoise piece.

8. Cut ½" x 4" fringe on each end of the pink fleece.

9. Insert the pillow form. Gather the fringe at the ends and tie with the pink fleece ties.

ROYAL BEACH PARTY

Three cheers for summer. It brings out the breezy in everything, like this swirly purple beach throw. Bordered with loopy knots, this throw is ideal for beach sitting or covering up on a cottage porch some chilly evening.

You'll need:
Fleece
  2 yds. lavender and purple print

Finished size: 44" x 54"

1. Cut the fleece 44" x 70".

2. Turn the edge of each short side up 8" and pin. See diagram below (A).

3. Cut ½" x 4" strips along the folded edge (B).

4. Tie the strips in knots to form loops (C).

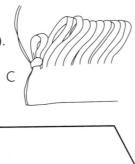

C

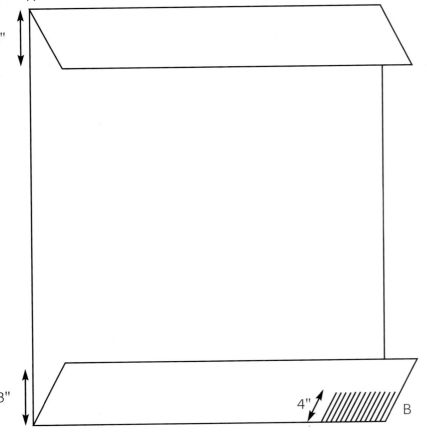

A

8"

8"

4"

B

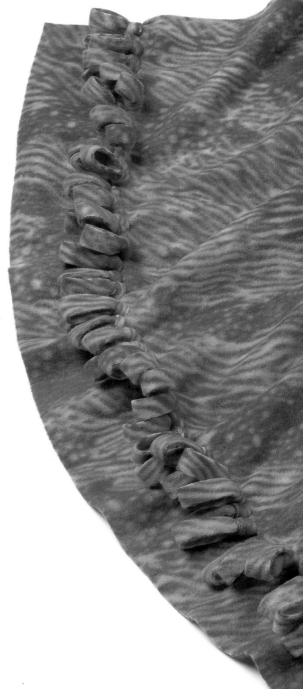

ROYAL PURPLE

You'll need:
Fleece:
  ⅔ yd. purple
  ¼ yd. lavender and purple print

Finished size: 16" x 16½"

1. Cut the purple fleece 17" x 33".

2. Cut two pieces of the print fleece 8½" x 17" for the tote. Cut a strip 3" x 43" of the print fleece for the straps.

3. Pin and sew the two short ends of the print fleece for the tote together using a ½" seam allowance.

4. Lay this piece on a flat surface with the wrong side facing up. Turn the edge of one long side up 4½" and pin along the top edge (see throw instructions on page 68).

5. Come in ¾" from the end and cut ½" x 1½" strips along the folded edge ending ¾" in from the opposite end.

6. Tie the strips in knots to form loops. Refer to the diagram on page 68.

7. Pin and sew the two remaining short ends together with a ½" seam allowance.

8. To make the tote: Fold the purple fleece in half with the edges of the short side meeting at the top. Pin and sew the sides together with a ½" seam allowance. Turn the tote right side out.

9. Pin and sew the right side of the fringed band to the wrong side of the purple tote along the top edge using a ½" seam allowance. Trim the seam and turn the band right side out.

10. For the strap: Fold the 3" x 43" strip of print fleece in half lengthwise.

11. Use a ¼" seam allowance and sew together on the long edge. Turn the strap right side out.

12. Pin the ends of the straps to the inside of the tote at the side seams and 2" down from the top edge. Sew to hold in place.

Bring along this beach tote and all your summer necessities including the beach throw. It's roomy enough for all these can't-live-without items. Constructed of a shocking purple fleece and topped with a swirly print bordered with loopy knots, this is one classy summer tote.

SPOT CHECK

Beachball pillows are a fun way for the children to relax during sunny summer play days. Cheerful polka dots combine with bright solids to create two sporty pillows for the kids to share. As a playroom accessory or just to toss on the bed for decoration, these pillows are sure to be popular with the youngsters. The matching throw doubles as a poolside coverup, or a throw for the bed.

Beach Ball #1
You'll need:
Fleece:
 ½ yd. orange
 ½ yd. pink
 ½ yd. polka dot

Beach Ball #2
You'll need:
Fleece
 ½ yd. lime green
 ½ yd. purple
 ½ yd. polka dot

1. For ball #1: Cut one piece of orange fleece, one of pink and two of polka dot 13" x 19". For ball #2: Cut one piece of lime green, one of purple and two of polka dot 13" x 19".

2. Fold each piece of fleece into fourths. Using the pattern on page 115, cut out the pillow pieces.

3. Pin and sew the sections together (see photo for color placement) leaving a 3" opening on one side.

4. Turn the ball right side out and stuff with fiberfill.

5. Hand sew the opening closed.

Beach Throw
You'll need:
Fleece:
 1 yd. polka dot fleece
Colorful foam beads
Plastic needle

Finished size: 30" x 58".

1. Cut the fleece 30" x 58"

2. Cut ½" x 3" fringe on each short end.

3. Use a large plastic needle to attach the beads to every other fringe strip. Thread the beads at various lengths for interest. Tie a knot right under the bead to secure.

POOLSIDE COMFORT

This fleece print features bandanna designs along with images of popular vacation spots. What an ideal fabric to create this soft and comfy cushion for a poolside chair. The plush touch of fleece provides plenty of comfort for summer guests.

You'll need:
Fleece:
  ¾ yd. summery print
  ¾ yd. red
2 bags of polyester fiberfill

1. Cut one piece of the summery print and one piece of the red 19" x 35".

2. Pin and sew together with right sides facing using a ½" seam allowance. Leave a 7" opening on one end.

3. Turn the cushion right side out and stuff with fiberfill. Hand sew the opening closed.

Tip:

We made this cushion reversible by using a print on one side and a solid on the other. You could also use a stripe with a solid or a floral print. Then, when you want to change the look of your patio furniture, simply reverse the cushions. If you want to make this cushion washable, use Velcro® strips to close the end. Make your own pillow form using muslin and fiberfill.

A SLICE OF SUMMER

Watermelon is always at its best enjoyed outdoors. This checkerboard throw, spread on the grass is the essential accessory for a summer picnic. Graphic appliqués of the season's favorite fruit emblazon this fleece throw lending an artistic presentation for any al fresco dining.

You'll need:
Fleece:
  2 yds. white
  1 yd. black   Steam-A-Seam2® fusible web
  ¼ yd. red   24 black buttons (assorted sizes)
  ⅛ yd. pink
  ½ yd. green   Finished size: 42" x 49"

1. Cut 15 black and 15 white 8" squares.

2. Cut one piece of white fleece 42" X 49".

3. To make the watermelon squares: Trace the pattern pieces (page 115) on pieces of Steam-A-Seam. Cut around the shapes and peel off the backing paper on one side. Apply the pieces to the appropriate fleece and cut out. Peel off the other backing paper and position the fleece pieces on the appropriate quilt squares. Trim pieces to fit squares (refer to the diagram).

4. With a pressing cloth over the top of the quilt square, iron the pieces in place. Check to see if all pieces are secure. If not, keep pressing until the proper bond is achieved. Repeat for all of the decorated squares.

5. Sew buttons to the watermelons as pictured.

6. For the quilt top, sew all the squares together (referring to the photograph) using a ½" seam allowance.

7. Lay the large piece of white fleece on a flat surface. Center the quilt top on the fleece. Pin and topstitch along all four edges.

8. Cut ½" x 3" fringe on all four sides of the white fleece.

TAKE A BREAK

You'll need:
Fleece
  2 yds. lime green
  1 yd. red
  1 yd. yellow
  1 yd. bright pink
  ½ yd. purple
3 to 4 bags polyester fiberfill

Finished size: 35" x 35"

1. Cut lime green, red, yellow and bright pink fabrics 25½" x 25½", then cut in half on the diagonal. You'll be using only half of each square. Save the other half for other projects.

2. Cut one piece of lime green fleece 36" x 36".

3. Cut four strips of purple fleece 4" x 36".

4. For the pillow top: Sew the sides of the triangles together using a ½" seam allowance. See photo for color placement.

5. Sew the short ends of all four purple strips together, using a ½" seam allowance.

6. With right sides facing, pin and sew one side of the purple strips to the pillow top.

7. Pin and sew the lime green fleece to the opposite side of the purple strip. Leave a 6" opening on one side to turn and stuff.

8. Turn the pillow right side out and stuff with fiberfill. Hand sew the opening closed.

Vibrant color triangles join together to form this jumbo-sized floor cushion. Or is it a bed for man's best friend? Whichever...it will certainly find a treasured spot in the house. The fuzzy fleece fabric makes it a popular choice for relaxing, sleeping or reading.

PLAYFUL PALS

Who's your favorite...Bright Eyed Bunny, Curious Kitty or Timid Teddy? The kids will want all three of these delightful stuffed animals. The off-the-wall colors will keep the kid's attention. The funny expressions will keep them laughing. Each one of these playful pals will be very well loved.

Teddy

You'll need:

Fleece:
- ⅓ yd. bright pink
- ⅓ yd. purple
- Scraps of lime green, turquoise, and white

Embroidery floss: black, turquoise, lime green, and white

Polyester fiberfill

Bunny

You'll need:

Fleece:
- ⅓ yd. lime green
- ⅓ yd. turquoise
- Scraps of bright pink, yellow, and white

Embroidery floss: black, pink, white, and yellow

Polyester fiberfill

Kitty

You'll need:

Fleece:
- ⅓ yd. turquoise
- ⅓ yd. yellow
- Scraps of lime green, bright pink, yellow, and purple

Embroidery floss: white, black, green, purple, yellow, and pink

Polyester fiberfill

1. Use the patterns on pages 118, 120-121 to cut out the appropriate fleece pieces.

2. For Teddy: Hand sew the inner ears, eyes and heart piece to the pink body using one strand of matching floss before sewing the body together.

3. For Bunny: Hand sew the inner ears, eyes and bow tie to the green body using one strand of matching floss.

4. For Kitty: Hand sew the eyes and polka dots to the body using one strand of matching floss.

5. For all: Stitch the nose using three strands of black floss and a satin stitch, and the mouth with a running stitch. In the center of the white eyes, stitch French knots using three strands of black floss.

6. Sew the body pieces together with right sides facing using a ¼" seam allowance. Leave a small opening for stuffing.

7. Turn the body right side out and stuff. Hand stitch the opening closed.

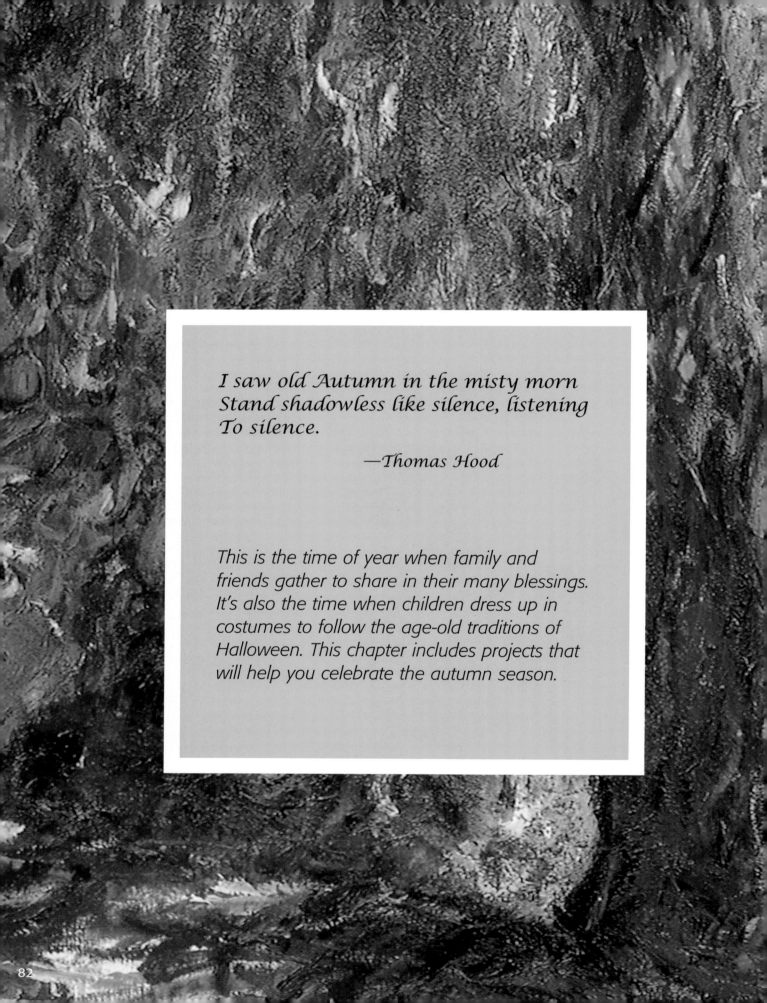

I saw old Autumn in the misty morn
Stand shadowless like silence, listening
To silence.

—Thomas Hood

This is the time of year when family and
friends gather to share in their many blessings.
It's also the time when children dress up in
costumes to follow the age-old traditions of
Halloween. This chapter includes projects that
will help you celebrate the autumn season.

AUTUMN

FRIGHT NIGHT

Harvest moons, scary black cats, jolly pumpkins and yummy candy corn decorate this happy Halloween quilt. Draped over a swing on the porch, this holiday quilt will serve as a welcoming sign for trick-or-treaters. Or hung on a wall above the buffet table, it will decorate the house during a Halloween party.

You'll need:
Fleece:
  1 1/2 yds. orange
  1/4 yd. black
  1/4 yd. bright yellow
  1/4 yd. pale yellow
  Scrap of white
  Scrap of green
Steam-A-Seam2® fusible web

Finished size: 33" x 40"

1. Cut one piece of orange fleece 33" x 40".

2. Cut seven black, six orange, and seven bright yellow pieces of fleece into 7 1/2" squares.

3. Use the patterns on pages 124 and 125 to trace appliqué pieces onto Steam-A-Seam.

4. Place the adhesive side of the pieces on the appropriate colors of fleece. Cut out the fleece pieces. Peel off the backing paper and iron to the appropriate square (refer to photograph).

5. For the quilt top: Sew the squares together using 1/2" seam allowance (refer to photo for placement).

6. Lay the large piece of orange fleece on a flat surface. Center the quilt top on the fleece. Pin and topstitch along all four edges.

7. Cut 1/2" x 3" fringe on all four sides of the orange fleece.

BABY'S FIRST HALLOWEEN

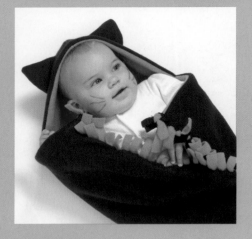

You'll need:

Fleece:
   1⅛ yds. orange
   1⅛ yds. black

Finished size: 30" x 40"

1. Cut one piece of orange fleece and one of black 36" x 43½".

2. Use the patterns on page 127 to cut out one orange hood, one black hood, and four black ears.

3. Fold the orange hood in half and sew from the front of the hood tapering off to the back (A). Repeat with the black hood.

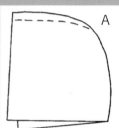

4. With right sides together, pin and machine stitch the two hood pieces together on the sides and across the top using a ⅜" seam allowance. Leave the bottom open for turning.

5. Turn the hood right side out.

6. Find the center of the orange fleece by folding the 36" side in half and marking with a pin.

7. Find the center back of the hood and pin to the center back of the orange fleece with the unfinished edges even. Sew in place using a ⅜" seam.

8. Place the black fleece on top of the orange with right sides together, matching edges.

9. Using a ½" seam allowance, stitch together at the top, starting 3" in from the edge and stopping 3" from the opposite side.

10. Turn right side out and again pin the bottom and sides together.

11. Clip the fringe around the sides and bottom ½" x 3". Tie the orange and black fringe together.

12. Sew the front ear to back ear using ¼" seam allowance. Clip seams and turn right side out. Repeat with the other ear.

13. Position the ears on the hood 1½" in from the front edge of the hood and 1½" from the center seam (refer to photo). Sew on the ears using ¼" seam allowance along the raw edge of the ear.

Note:
When sewing on the ears, use black thread on the top and orange thread in bobbin to match the fleece.

Who says she's too young to go trick-or-treating? Wrap her up in this blanket/costume and she's ready to join her brothers and sisters on the Halloween trek through the neighborhood. She might need to be carried by Mom or Dad, but she's certainly going to enjoy the event just as much as the older kids.

Having a Halloween bash? How about whipping up some fun favors to hand out to departing guests? These fleece bags are simple to make—and are big enough to hold lots of tasty treats. The holiday images are cut out of fleece and ironed onto the bags. Colorful beads add the final touch to tie up these bags with a flourish.

TRICK
-OR-
TREAT

You'll need:
Fleece:
  ½ yd. black
  ½ yd. orange
  Scrap of yellow
  Scrap of white
8 pony beads: orange and black
Pinking shears
Steam-A-Seam2® fusible web

Finished size: 7" x 12"

1. With pinking shears, cut two pieces of black fleece and two pieces of orange, 7½" x 13".

2. Use the patterns on page 124 to trace the Halloween shapes onto one side of the Steam-A-Seam. Cut around the shapes, then peel off the backing paper. Apply the shapes, adhesive-side-down on the appropriate color of fleece. Cut out the shapes. Lay aside.

3. Sew the black fleece together on one short end and along both long sides using a ½" seam allowance. Repeat with the orange fleece.

4. Turn the bags right side out. Peel off the backing paper of the cut out fleece shapes and apply to the appropriate bags. With a pressing cloth over the top, iron the shapes to the bags.

5. Use pinking shears to cut four ½" x 10" ties (two black, one orange and one yellow).

6. Add a bead to each end of the ties and secure with a knot. Tie two ties around the top of each bag.

PUMPKIN PATCH

The buffet for your Thanksgiving dinner needs some clever decoration. These plump fleece pumpkins will certainly add a holiday flair to the event. After dinner, use these symbols of the season to decorate a couch or bench.

You'll need:
Fleece:
  ½ yd. burnt orange
  Scrap of green
  Scrap of brown
Polyester fiberfill
Craft glue

1. Use the pattern on page 122 to cut the orange pumpkin sections and the pattern on page 123 for the green leaves.

2. With right sides facing, sew sections of the pumpkin together using a ½" seam allowance, leaving an opening on one side. Turn right side out.

3. Stuff with fiberfill and hand stitch the opening closed.

4. Hand sew or glue the "leaves" on top of the pumpkin.

5. Cut a piece of brown fleece 2" x 2". Roll it up into a "stem" and glue together along one side. Glue or tack the stem to the center of the leaves.

Tip:

As a special gift for your guests at a holiday luncheon, make mini-pumpkin pincushions. Reduce the patterns to your desired size, sew according to the above instructions, then stuff very firmly with fiberfill.

Or personalize the mini-pumpkins with your guest's names and use as place cards at each place setting.

To personalize, tie a tag with the person's name around the stem of the pumpkin. Use thin green wire to tie the tag on and curl it slightly to resemble the trendrils of the pumpkin.

HARVEST OF PILLOWS

These images of the harvest charmingly line a sofa. Each shaped pillow looks good enough to eat—a rosy red tomato, curly topped carrot, leafy green pepper, and hot and spicy chili pepper. Displayed on your couch, they're certain to become conversation starters.

Tomato

You'll need:
Fleece:
  ¼ yd. red
  Scrap of green
Polyester fiberfill
Craft glue

1. Use the patterns on page 122 and 123 to cut out the tomato and leaf pieces. Cut out four red pieces and the green leaf piece. Cut a piece of green fleece 1" x 2" for the stem.

2. Sew the red pieces together using a ¼" seam allowance. Leave an opening on one side to turn and stuff.

3. Turn the tomato right side out and stuff with fiberfill. Hand sew the opening closed.

4. Glue or tack at the center of the leaves to the top of the tomato.

5. Roll the 1" x 2" piece and glue along the 1" side to make the stem. Glue or tack the stem to the center of the leaves.

Carrot

You'll need:
Fleece:
  ¼ yd. orange
  ¼ yd. green
Polyester fiberfill

1. Use the pattern on page 123 to cut three sections of the orange fleece.

2. Sew all three pieces together along the long sides using a ¼" seam allowance. Turn right side out.

3. Cut a piece of green fleece to fit around the top edge of the carrot, approximately 5" x 16½".

4. Pin the green fleece along the top edge of the carrot, overlapping the orange fleece ½".

5. Topstitch along the bottom edge of the green fleece and again ½" up from the first stitch line.

6. Cut ½" x 4½" fringe of the green fleece.

7. Fill the pillow with fiberfill. Gather the top together and tie with a strip of green fleece ½" x 18".

8. Curl the fringe and the tie.

Green Pepper

You'll need:
Fleece:
  ¼ yd. green
  Scrap of light green
Polyester fiberfill
Craft glue

1. Use the patterns on page 122 to cut the green pepper pieces. Use the round pattern on page 122 an pinking shears to cut the light gree cap. Cut a piece of the light green fleece 1½" x 2" for the stem.

2. Sew all six pieces together using

a ¼" seam allowance. Leave an opening on one side to turn and stuff.

3. Turn the pepper right side out. Stuff with fiberfill and hand sew the opening closed. To give the pepper a less round shape, take a stitch all the way through the pillow and pull tightly. Knot.

4. Glue or tack the light green cap to the top of the pepper.

5. Roll the 1½" x 2" piece of fleece and glue along the 1½" edge to form the stem. Glue to the center of the cap.

Chili Pepper

You'll need:
Fleece:
  ⅛ yd. red
  Scrap of green
Polyester fiberfill
Craft glue

1. Use the pattern on pages 122 and 123 to cut out four pieces of red fleece for the chili pepper and the leaves from the green fleece.

2. Cut a piece of green fleece 2" x 2" for the stem.

3. Sew all four pieces of the chili pepper together using a ¼" seam allowance. Leave an opening on one side to turn and stuff.

4. Turn the chili pepper right side out. Stuff with fiberfill and hand stitch the opening closed.

5. Glue or tack the leaves to the top.

6. Roll the 2" x 2" green fleece and glue along one edge to form a stem. Glue or tack the stem to the center of the leaves.

FALLING LEAVES

We want to catch and capture leaves forever—saving each exquisite shape as they flutter away. Now we can, in a richness of leaf-patterned design that brings beauty and autumn color into any room of the house. This handsome throw displays autumn leaves cascading down the panels of autumn-colored fleece.

You'll need:
Fleece:
 ½ yd. green
 ½ yd. tan
 ½ yd. brown
 ¼ yd. autumn print
Steam-A-Seam2® fusible web
Embroidery floss: tan, orange and green

Finished size: 44½" x 56"

1. Cut the green, tan, and brown fleece into 15½" x 56" panels.

2. Trace the leaf designs on Steam-A-Seam using the patterns on pages 123, 124 & 125. Place the adhesive side of the leaf pieces on the autumn print fleece and cut out the leaves.

3. Peel off the backing paper and with a pressing cloth on top, iron the leaves to each color panel (referring to the photo).

4. Sew the three panels together using a ½" seam allowance with the tan fleece in the center.

5. Blanket stitch around the outside edge of the throw using six strands of embroidery floss. Alternate colors of floss for each colored panel.

FALL FASHIONS

Fleece is available in such a wide variety of solids and prints. But it's also available in more fashionable styles, such as embossed and embroidered varieties. These two fabrics have been combined to create this easy-to-make, comfortable, yet chic jacket and scarf duet. The jacket is of a plush and embossed fleece and sews up in a minute with just two seams and no hems. The scarf is a colorfully embroidered fleece that coordinates so nicely with the jacket. It's fringed and tied at each end for a dazzling finish.

Jacket

You'll need:
Fleece:
  2 yds. red embossed

To fit sizes 10/12 (approximately)
Finished length: 24½"

1. Use the diagram below to make a paper pattern for the jacket.

2. Pin the pattern to the fleece and cut out jacket according to the diagram.

3. Fold the jacket piece along the shoulder line with right sides together and stitch the underarm and side seams using a ½" seam allowance. Clip the corners. Press the seams open.

4. Stay stitch around the neckline, down the front and along the bottom about ⅛" in from the edges.

5. Turn up the sleeves to form a cuff.

Scarf

You'll need:
Fleece:
  ⅓ yd. red embossed
  ⅓ yd. black embroidered

Finished size: 8" x 54"

1. Cut the embossed fleece and black fleece 9" x 58".

2. With right sides facing, sew the two pieces together using a ½" seam allowance. Start sewing 4" up from one short end and stop 4" from the opposite end.

3. Trim the seams and turn the scarf right side out.

4. Cut fringe on both short ends ¾" x 4". Tie the front and back fringe together with a double knot.

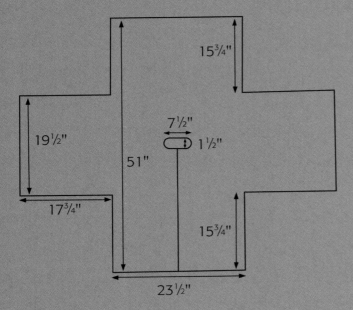

AUTUMN SONATA

Autumn leaves and the colors of fall are the inspiration for this clever no-sew pillow. The fleece fringe simply ties this pillow together, and in only a few minutes you have a handsome addition to your sofa.

You'll need:
Fleece:
  ⅔ yd. brown
  ⅔ yd. burnt orange
  ⅔ yd. autumn print
14" pillow form

Finished size: 14" x 14"

1. For pillow front: Use the pattern on page 125 to cut one piece of burnt orange and one of brown.

2. For pillow back: Cut the autumn print 20" x 20".

3. Cut ¼" x 3" fringe on all sides of each pillow piece.

4. Tie the center section of the brown and orange pieces together.

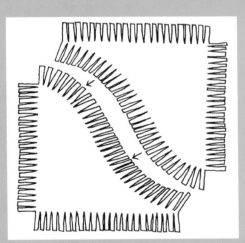
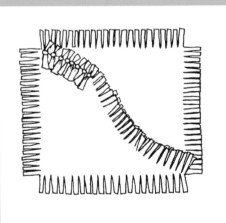

5. Place the tied front piece on the print backing piece with wrong sides together. Tie the fringe together on three sides.

6. Insert the pillow form. Tie the fringe on the fourth side to close.

FLEECE FOR FALL

Autumn is a time of rainy days with a brisk chill in the air. A time to sit by the fire, relax and read. When we sense this change in the season, we can allow ourselves a little redecorating. This lovely pillow with its dramatic drawnwork design fits in this romantic picture perfectly. Its burnt orange covering reminiscent of autumn leaves, displays the burgundy fleece beneath. The soft, luxurious fleece combined with the fall colors makes this pillow the ideal makeover solution to transition from summer to fall.

You'll need:
Fleece:
 ¾ yd. burnt orange
 ¾ yd. burgundy
18" pillow form

Finished size: 18" x 18"

1. Cut one piece of burnt orange and two pieces of burgundy fleece each 19" x 19". Cut 20 strips of orange ¼" x 4" for ties.

2. Lay the orange fleece on a flat surface. Following the diagram, mark where the cuts are to be made (dashed lines on diagram represent folds). Fold each side up 4" and start cutting 6" from each end. Cut 1½" slits every ¼" on the fold.

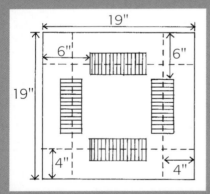 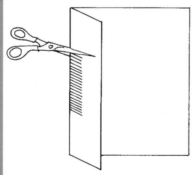

3. Sew one piece of the burgundy fleece to the back of the orange along all four sides. Use a ½" seam allowance. This forms the top of the pillow.

4. Sew three sides of the pillow top to the second piece of the burgundy fleece with right sides together using a ½" seam allowance. Trim seams and turn right side out.

5. Insert the pillow form and hand sew the opening closed.

6. Tie three slits together in each section on the orange fleece. Trim ties.

STADIUM TOTE

You'll cheer your team to victory as you sit in warm comfort under your fleece throw. Designed in your school colors and fitting so nicely in the matching tote, this combo will make stadium seating a snap. The tote is cleverly embellished with your team's pennant purchased from the school bookstore. It becomes not only a symbol of your alma mater, but the closure that holds everything together.

Stadium Tote

You'll need:
Fleece:
  ¾ yd. royal blue
25" school pennant

Finished size: 18" x 24"

1. Cut the blue fleece 19" x 28½".

2. Fold the short end of the fleece up toward the opposite end stopping ½" from the edge.

3. Pin the sides and sew together using a ½" seam allowance. Trim the seams and turn right side out.

4. Lay the top edge of the pennant to the extended top edge of the tote. Topstitch ½" from the edge. Fold the pennant over to form a flap.

5. Optional: Add Velcro strips to close the pouch.

Stadium Throw

You'll need:
Fleece:
  1½ yds. blue

1. Cut the blue fleece 48" x 60". Fringe the edges of the throw ½" x 4". Insert in the pouch.

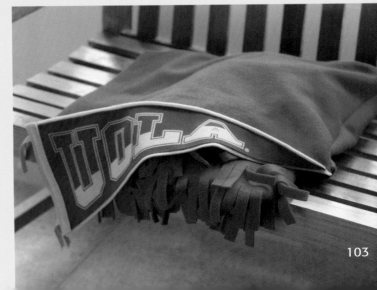

WITH A TWIST

You'll while away autumn evenings nestled into your comfortable couch relaxing against this soft pillow. Decorated with twisted strips of autumn-hued fleece, this unusual pillow is just right for dreaming of seasons yet to come.

You'll need:
Fleece:
  ½ yd. black
  ⅛ yd. each light green, dark green, orange, red, and brown
Polyester fiberfill

Finished size: 15" x 17"

1. Cut two pieces of black fleece 16" x 18" each. Cut strips of light green, dark green, orange, red and brown fleece 3" x 18".

2. Following the diagram, position the strips on one piece of the black fleece along one side. Pin and stay stitch in place (A).

3. Place a ruler diagonally across strips where shown and mark. Refer to the diagram (B). Pin and sew across marked line.

4. Remove pins and twist each strip once, beneath the stitching. Pin strips again to the edge of the pillow top and stay stitch in place (C). Remove pins.

5. With right sides together, sew the front and back pieces together using a ½" seam allowance. Leave an opening at one side for stuffing. Trim seams and turn right side out.

6. Stuff the pillow with fiberfill and hand sew the opening closed.

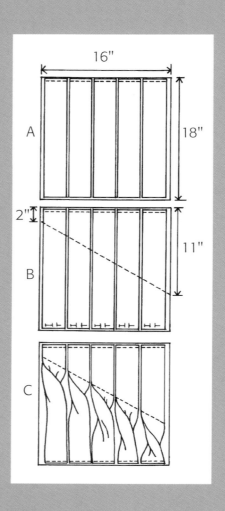

FALL INTO AUTUMN

Wheeee!! What fun. Teddy has jumped into the pile of leaves, just as we used to do as kids. You can almost smell the aromatic smoke coming from the chimneys of nearby fireplaces. There's a hint of winter in the air and you realize it's almost time for Christmas. Any child would love to receive a gift as cute as this stuffed teddy.

You'll need:

Fleece:
  1/8 yd. brown
  Scrap of beige

Embroidery floss: black and white
Brown buttons: 2 medium, 2 large
Upholstery needle

1. Use the patterns on page 126 to cut out the fleece for the bear.

2. With right sides facing and using a 1/4" seam allowance, sew the center front seam from the lower edge to the dot. Press the seam open.

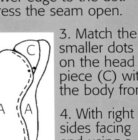

3. Match the smaller dots on the head piece (C) with the dots on the body front (A).

4. With right sides facing and using a 1/4" seam allowance, sew the center back seam together from the lower edge to the dot. Press the seam open.

5. For each ear: Sew one brown and one beige piece together between the asterisk leaving the bottom open. Turn right side out.

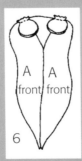

6. Use a gathering stitch along the bottom edge of the ears. Gather to fit between the asterisks on the front piece (A), with edges matching and the ear toward the center. Stay stitch in place.

7. With right sides facing, match the back seam to the large dot on C, and the sides and bottom edges of A and B. Pin and sew together leaving an opening toward the bottom.

8. Turn right side out and stuff with fiberfill. Hand stitch the opening closed.

9. Sew the arm and leg pieces together leaving openings for stuffing. Turn right side out, stuff and hand sew the opening closed.

10. Use an upholstery needle and strong thread to attach the medium buttons and arms to the bear's body.

11. Repeat step 10 to sew on the legs, using the larger buttons.

12. Using black embroidery floss, stitch the eyes, nose and mouth (marked on pattern). Add a dot of white embroidery floss to make a highlight in the eyes.

13. Tie an autumn colored bow around the neck. Pull tightly to form an indentation for the neck.

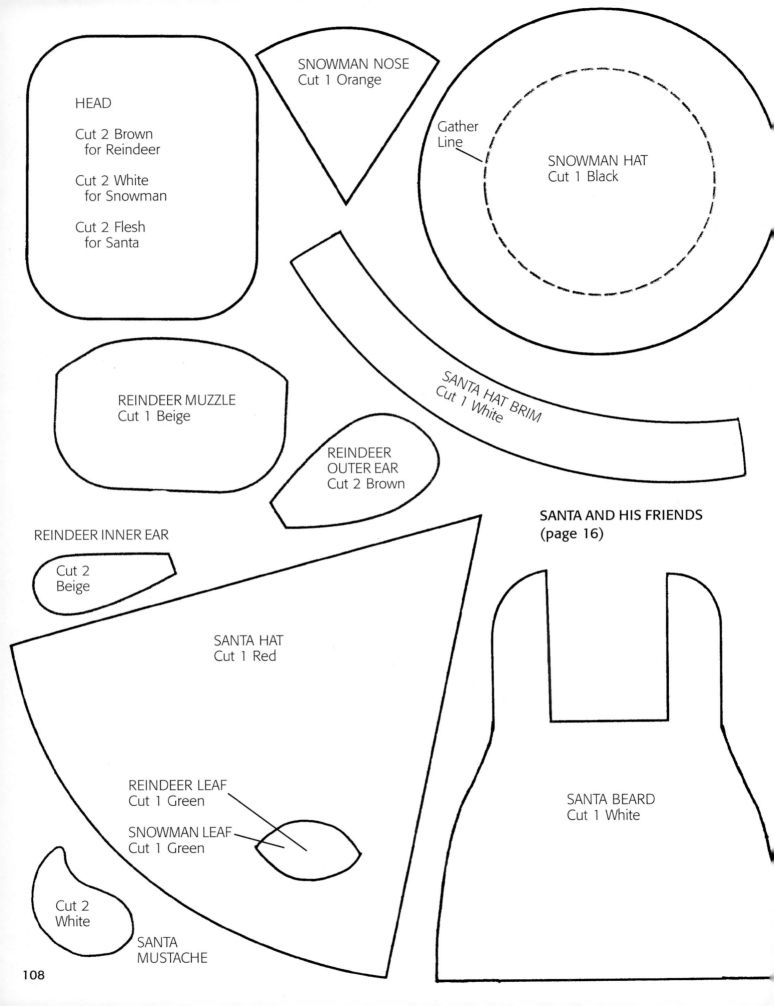

HEAD

Cut 2 Brown
 for Reindeer

Cut 2 White
 for Snowman

Cut 2 Flesh
 for Santa

SNOWMAN NOSE
Cut 1 Orange

Gather
Line

SNOWMAN HAT
Cut 1 Black

REINDEER MUZZLE
Cut 1 Beige

SANTA HAT BRIM
Cut 1 White

REINDEER
OUTER EAR
Cut 2 Brown

REINDEER INNER EAR

Cut 2
Beige

SANTA AND HIS FRIENDS
(page 16)

SANTA HAT
Cut 1 Red

REINDEER LEAF
Cut 1 Green

SNOWMAN LEAF
Cut 1 Green

SANTA BEARD
Cut 1 White

Cut 2
White

SANTA
MUSTACHE

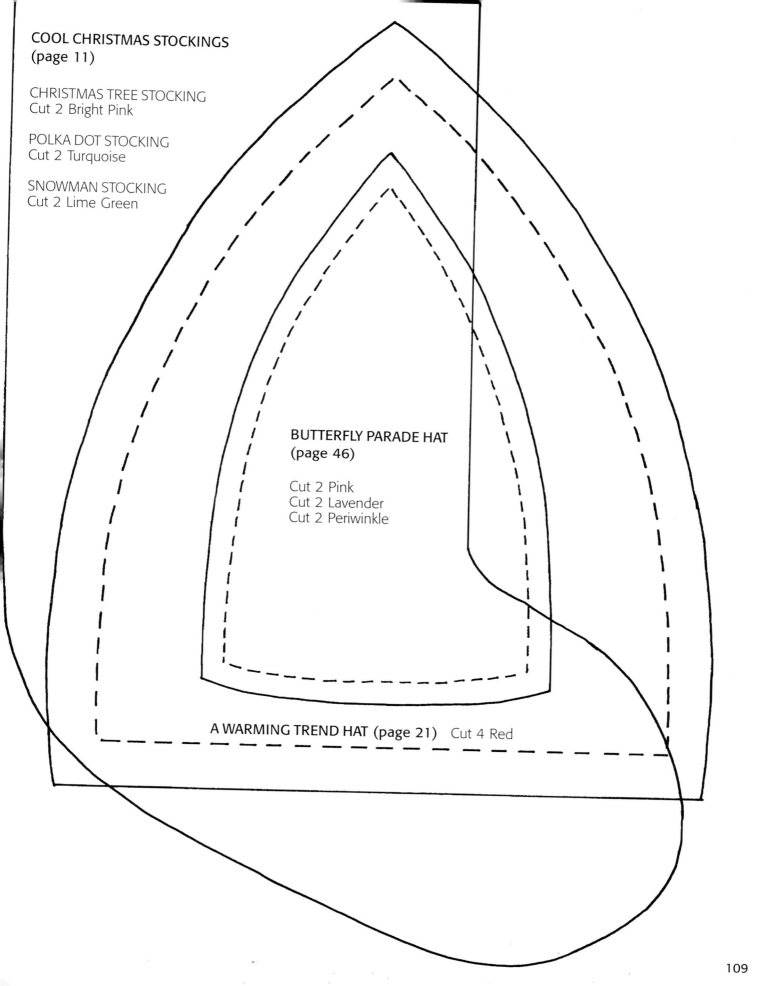

COOL CHRISTMAS STOCKINGS
(page 11)

CHRISTMAS TREE STOCKING
Cut 2 Bright Pink

POLKA DOT STOCKING
Cut 2 Turquoise

SNOWMAN STOCKING
Cut 2 Lime Green

BUTTERFLY PARADE HAT
(page 46)

Cut 2 Pink
Cut 2 Lavender
Cut 2 Periwinkle

A WARMING TREND HAT (page 21)   Cut 4 Red

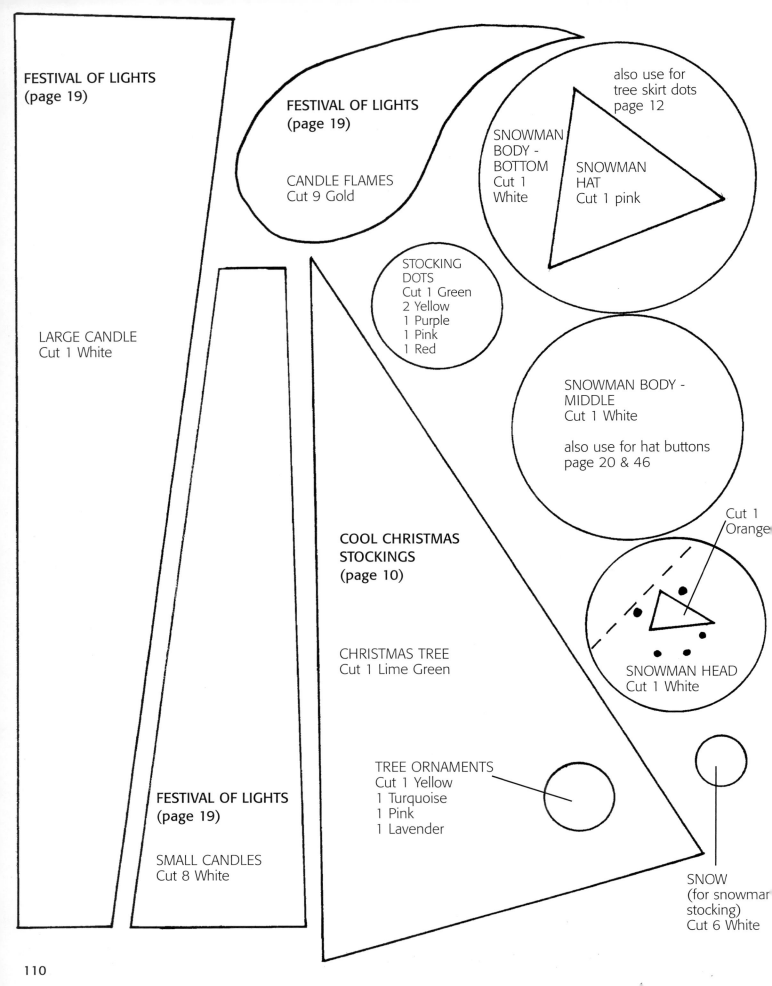

FESTIVAL OF LIGHTS
(page 19)

FESTIVAL OF LIGHTS
(page 19)

CANDLE FLAMES
Cut 9 Gold

also use for
tree skirt dots
page 12

SNOWMAN
BODY -
BOTTOM
Cut 1
White

SNOWMAN
HAT
Cut 1 pink

LARGE CANDLE
Cut 1 White

STOCKING
DOTS
Cut 1 Green
2 Yellow
1 Purple
1 Pink
1 Red

SNOWMAN BODY -
MIDDLE
Cut 1 White

also use for hat buttons
page 20 & 46

Cut 1
Orange

**COOL CHRISTMAS
STOCKINGS**
(page 10)

SNOWMAN HEAD
Cut 1 White

CHRISTMAS TREE
Cut 1 Lime Green

FESTIVAL OF LIGHTS
(page 19)

TREE ORNAMENTS
Cut 1 Yellow
1 Turquoise
1 Pink
1 Lavender

SMALL CANDLES
Cut 8 White

SNOW
(for snowmar
stocking)
Cut 6 White

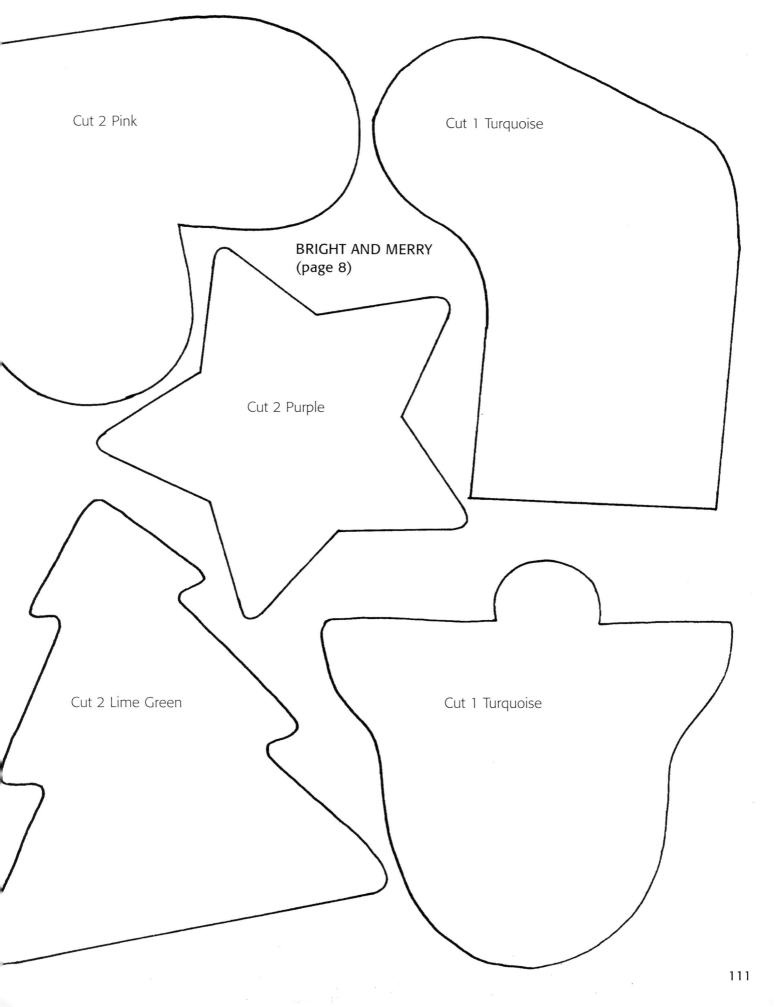

Cut 2 Pink

Cut 1 Turquoise

BRIGHT AND MERRY
(page 8)

Cut 2 Purple

Cut 2 Lime Green

Cut 1 Turquoise

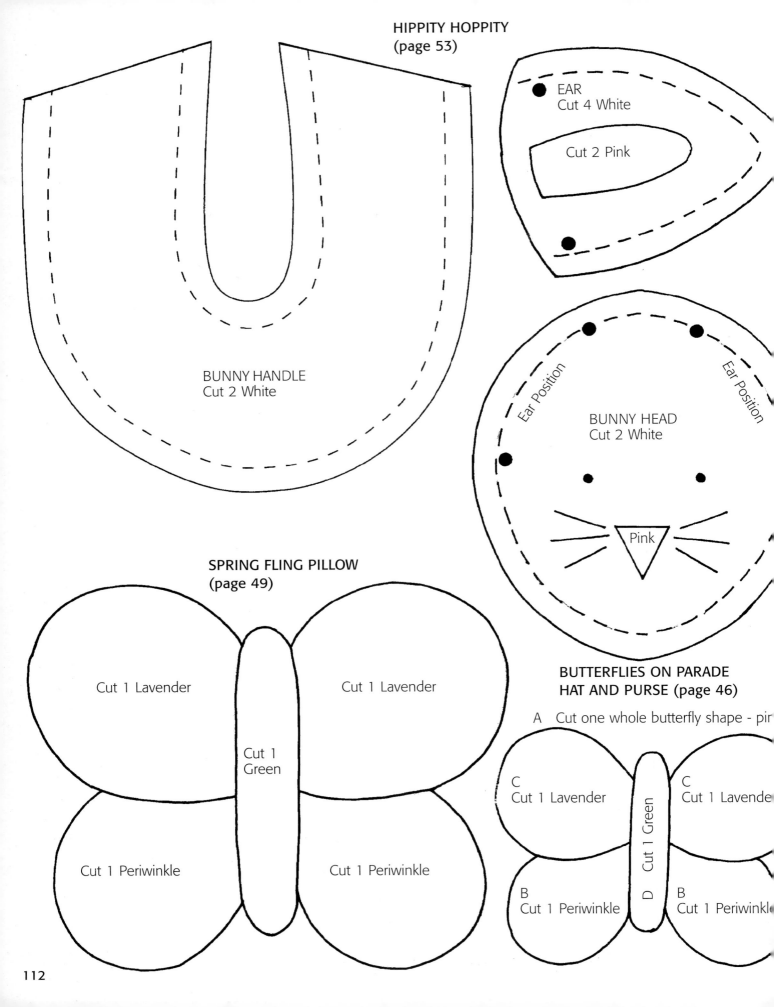

HIPPITY HOPPITY
(page 53)

EAR
Cut 4 White

Cut 2 Pink

BUNNY HANDLE
Cut 2 White

Ear Position

Ear Position

BUNNY HEAD
Cut 2 White

Pink

SPRING FLING PILLOW
(page 49)

Cut 1 Lavender

Cut 1 Lavender

Cut 1
Green

Cut 1 Periwinkle

Cut 1 Periwinkle

BUTTERFLIES ON PARADE
HAT AND PURSE (page 46)

A   Cut one whole butterfly shape - pir

C
Cut 1 Lavender

C
Cut 1 Lavende

D Cut 1 Green

B
Cut 1 Periwinkle

B
Cut 1 Periwinkle

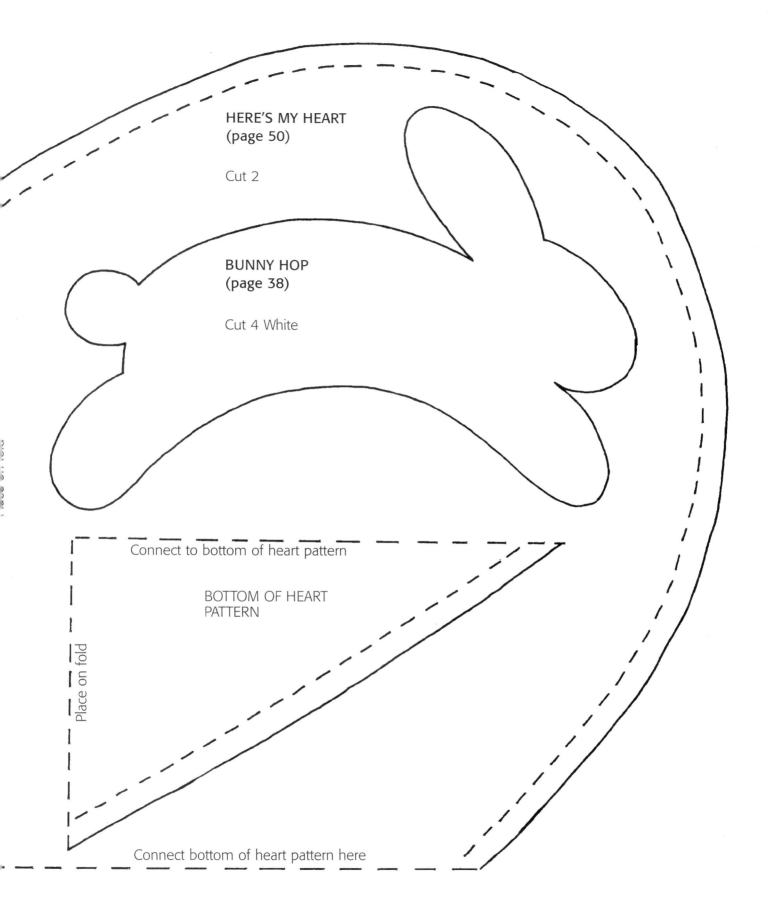

HERE'S MY HEART
(page 50)

Cut 2

BUNNY HOP
(page 38)

Cut 4 White

Connect to bottom of heart pattern

BOTTOM OF HEART
PATTERN

Place on fold

Connect bottom of heart pattern here

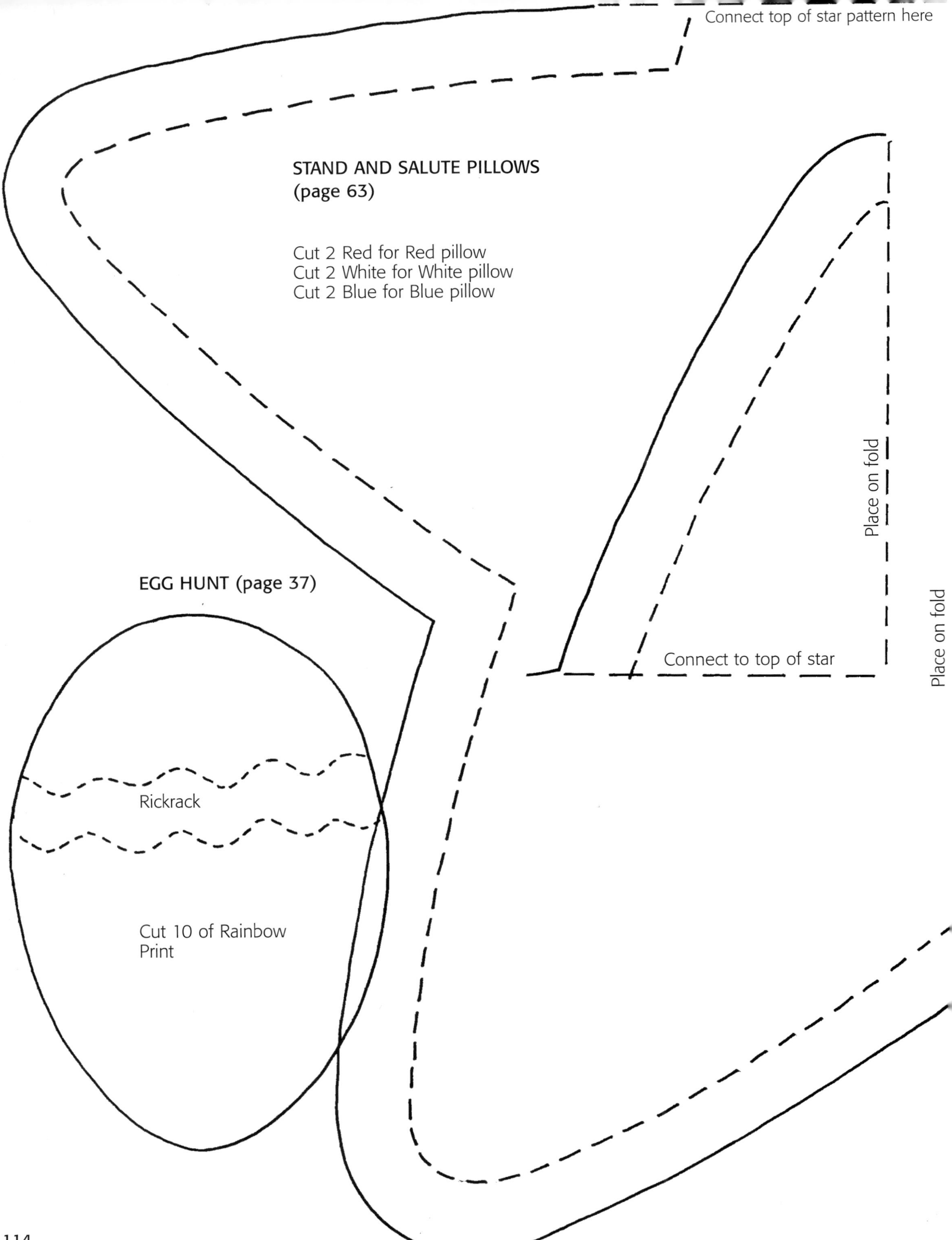

Connect top of star pattern here

STAND AND SALUTE PILLOWS
(page 63)

Cut 2 Red for Red pillow
Cut 2 White for White pillow
Cut 2 Blue for Blue pillow

Place on fold

Place on fold

Connect to top of star

EGG HUNT (page 37)

Rickrack

Cut 10 of Rainbow
Print

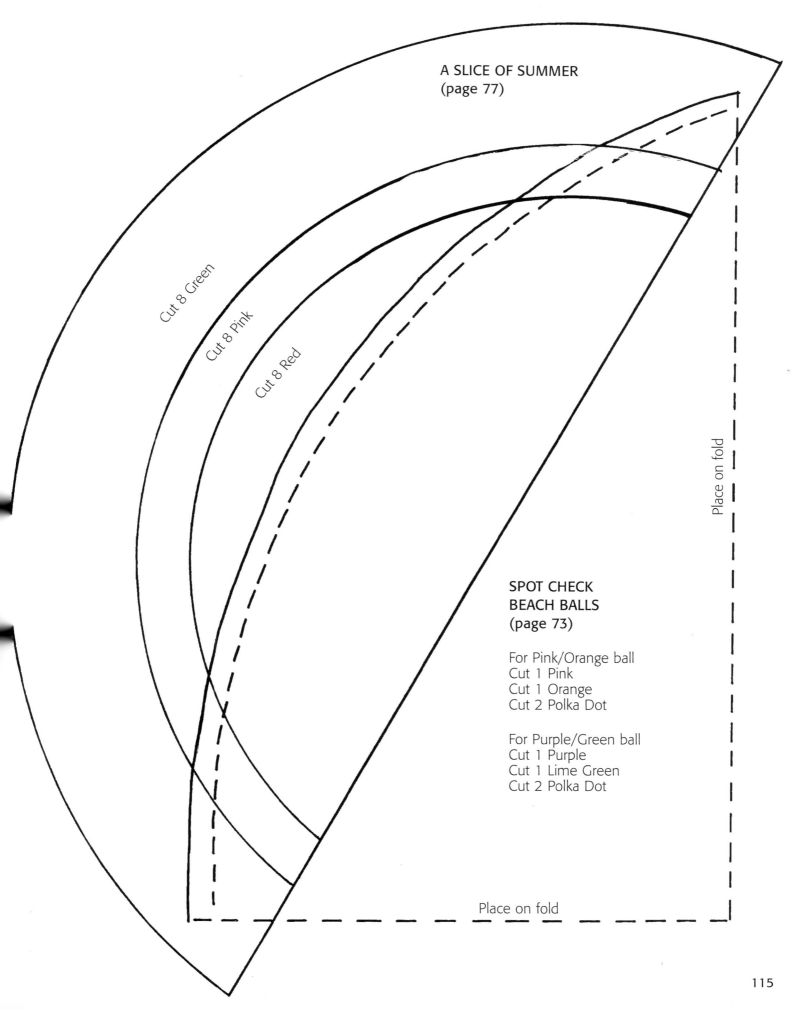

A SLICE OF SUMMER
(page 77)

Cut 8 Green

Cut 8 Pink

Cut 8 Red

Place on fold

SPOT CHECK
BEACH BALLS
(page 73)

For Pink/Orange ball
Cut 1 Pink
Cut 1 Orange
Cut 2 Polka Dot

For Purple/Green ball
Cut 1 Purple
Cut 1 Lime Green
Cut 2 Polka Dot

Place on fold

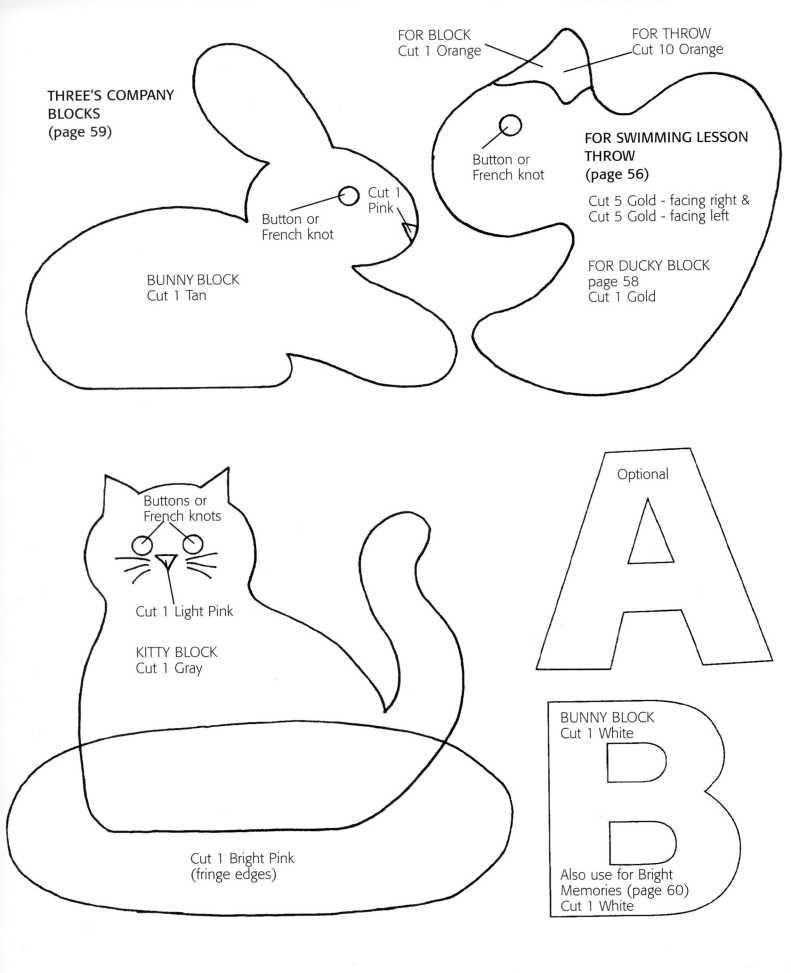

THREE'S COMPANY BLOCKS (page 59)

FOR BLOCK
Cut 1 Orange

FOR THROW
Cut 10 Orange

Button or
French knot

FOR SWIMMING LESSON THROW
(page 56)

Cut 5 Gold - facing right &
Cut 5 Gold - facing left

FOR DUCKY BLOCK
page 58
Cut 1 Gold

Cut 1
Pink

Button or
French knot

BUNNY BLOCK
Cut 1 Tan

Buttons or
French knots

Cut 1 Light Pink

KITTY BLOCK
Cut 1 Gray

Cut 1 Bright Pink
(fringe edges)

Optional

BUNNY BLOCK
Cut 1 White

Also use for Bright
Memories (page 60)
Cut 1 White

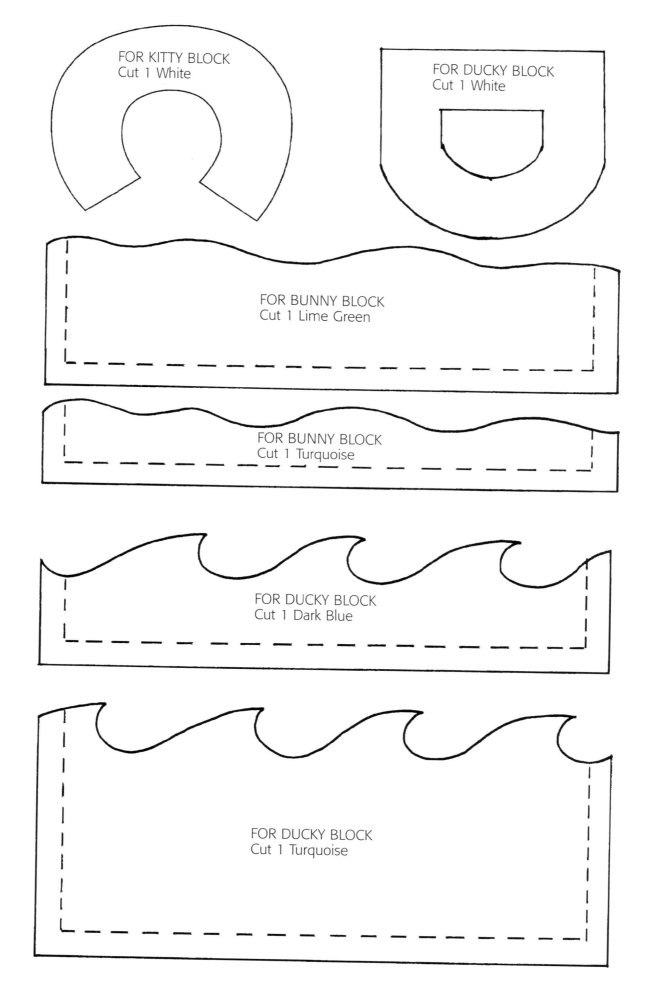

FOR KITTY BLOCK
Cut 1 White

FOR DUCKY BLOCK
Cut 1 White

FOR BUNNY BLOCK
Cut 1 Lime Green

FOR BUNNY BLOCK
Cut 1 Turquoise

FOR DUCKY BLOCK
Cut 1 Dark Blue

FOR DUCKY BLOCK
Cut 1 Turquoise

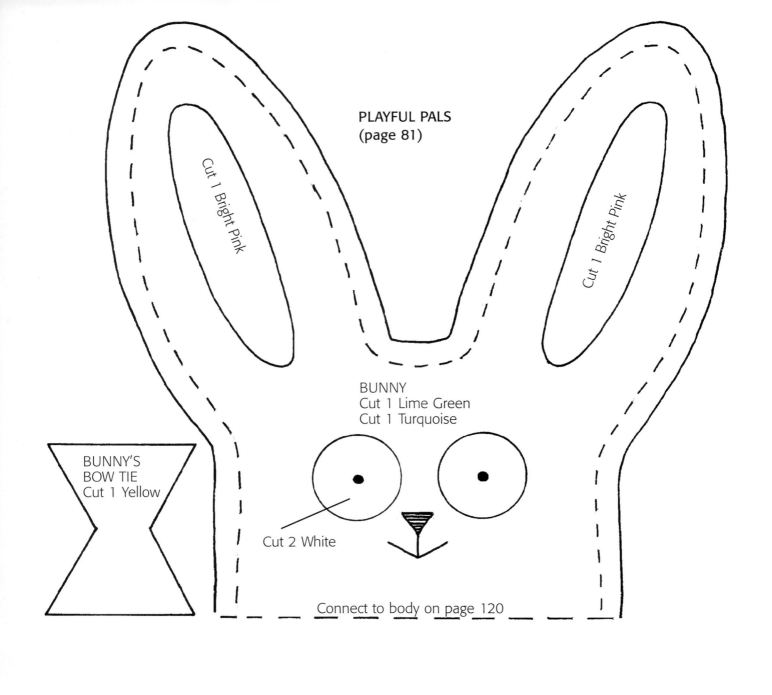

PLAYFUL PALS
(page 81)

Cut 1 Bright Pink

Cut 1 Bright Pink

BUNNY
Cut 1 Lime Green
Cut 1 Turquoise

BUNNY'S
BOW TIE
Cut 1 Yellow

Cut 2 White

Connect to body on page 120

SWIMMING LESSONS
(page 56)

Cut 3 Turquoise

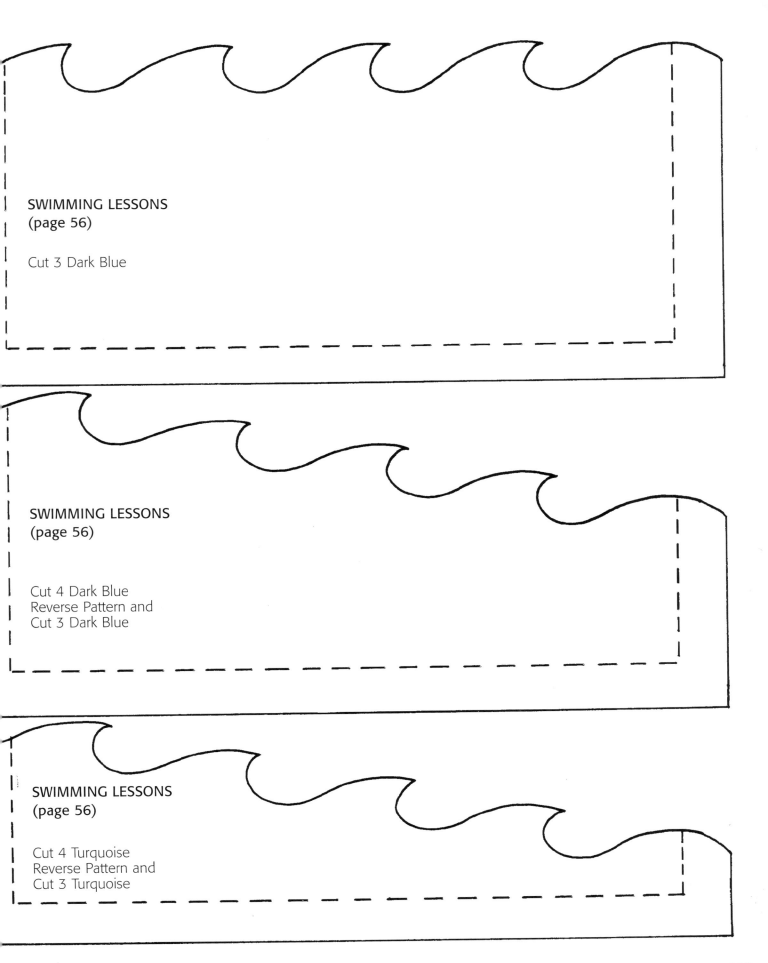

SWIMMING LESSONS
(page 56)

Cut 3 Dark Blue

SWIMMING LESSONS
(page 56)

Cut 4 Dark Blue
Reverse Pattern and
Cut 3 Dark Blue

SWIMMING LESSONS
(page 56)

Cut 4 Turquoise
Reverse Pattern and
Cut 3 Turquoise

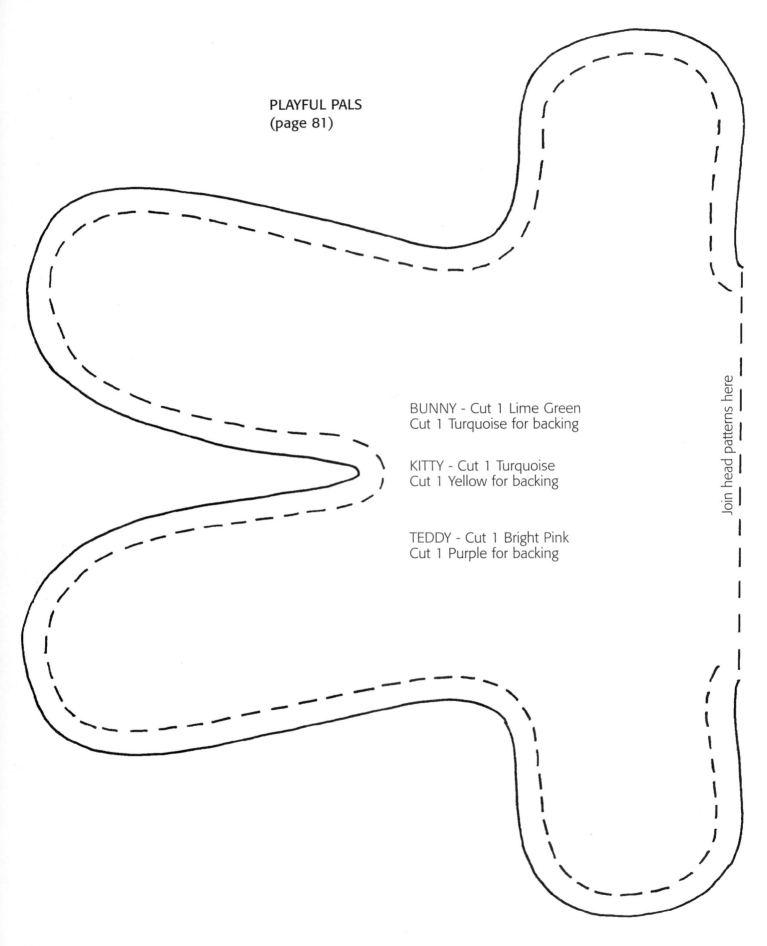

PLAYFUL PALS
(page 81)

BUNNY - Cut 1 Lime Green
Cut 1 Turquoise for backing

KITTY - Cut 1 Turquoise
Cut 1 Yellow for backing

TEDDY - Cut 1 Bright Pink
Cut 1 Purple for backing

Join head patterns here

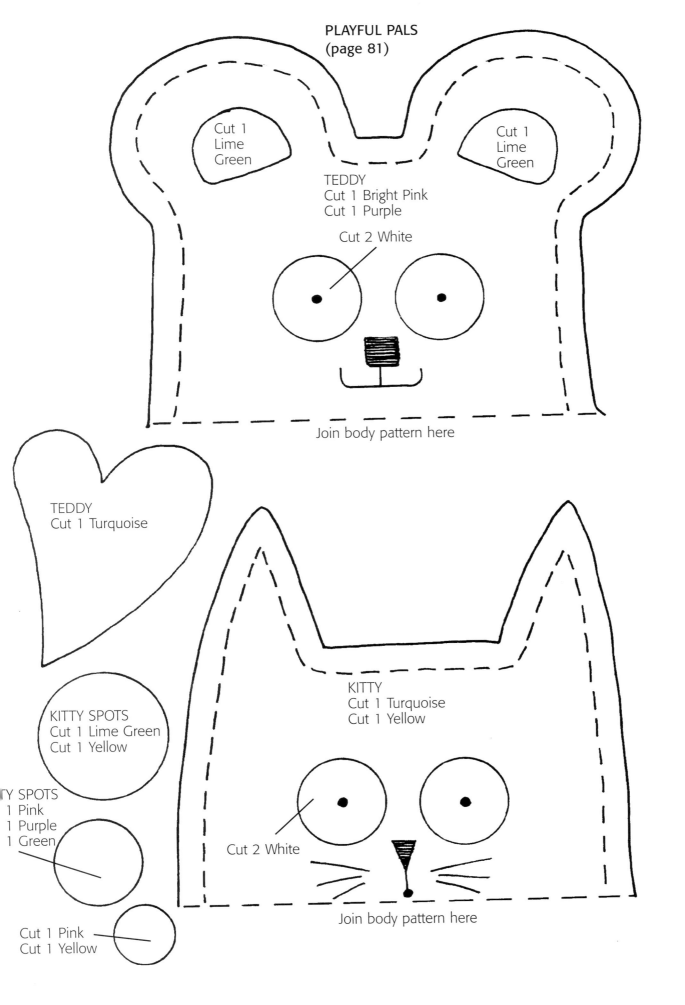

PLAYFUL PALS
(page 81)

Cut 1
Lime
Green

Cut 1
Lime
Green

TEDDY
Cut 1 Bright Pink
Cut 1 Purple

Cut 2 White

Join body pattern here

TEDDY
Cut 1 Turquoise

KITTY
Cut 1 Turquoise
Cut 1 Yellow

KITTY SPOTS
Cut 1 Lime Green
Cut 1 Yellow

Y SPOTS
1 Pink
1 Purple
1 Green

Cut 2 White

Cut 1 Pink
Cut 1 Yellow

Join body pattern here

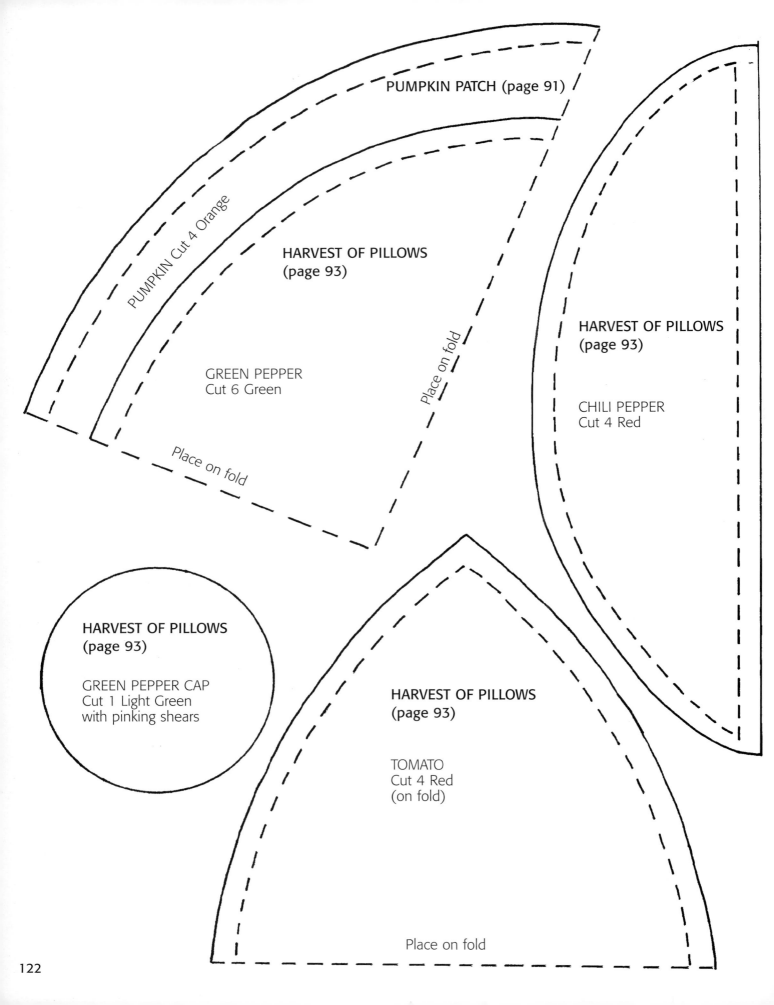

PUMPKIN PATCH (page 91)

PUMPKIN Cut 4 Orange

HARVEST OF PILLOWS
(page 93)

GREEN PEPPER
Cut 6 Green

Place on fold

Place on fold

HARVEST OF PILLOWS
(page 93)

CHILI PEPPER
Cut 4 Red

HARVEST OF PILLOWS
(page 93)

GREEN PEPPER CAP
Cut 1 Light Green
with pinking shears

HARVEST OF PILLOWS
(page 93)

TOMATO
Cut 4 Red
(on fold)

Place on fold

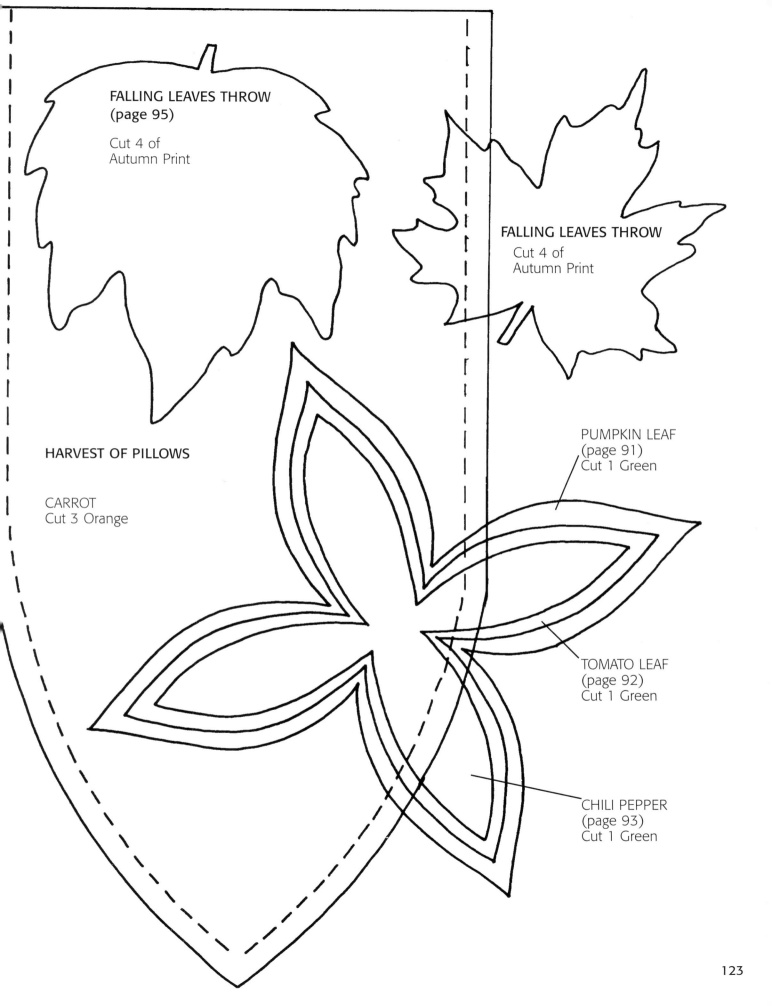

FALLING LEAVES THROW
(page 95)

Cut 4 of
Autumn Print

FALLING LEAVES THROW

Cut 4 of
Autumn Print

HARVEST OF PILLOWS

CARROT
Cut 3 Orange

PUMPKIN LEAF
(page 91)
Cut 1 Green

TOMATO LEAF
(page 92)
Cut 1 Green

CHILI PEPPER
(page 93)
Cut 1 Green

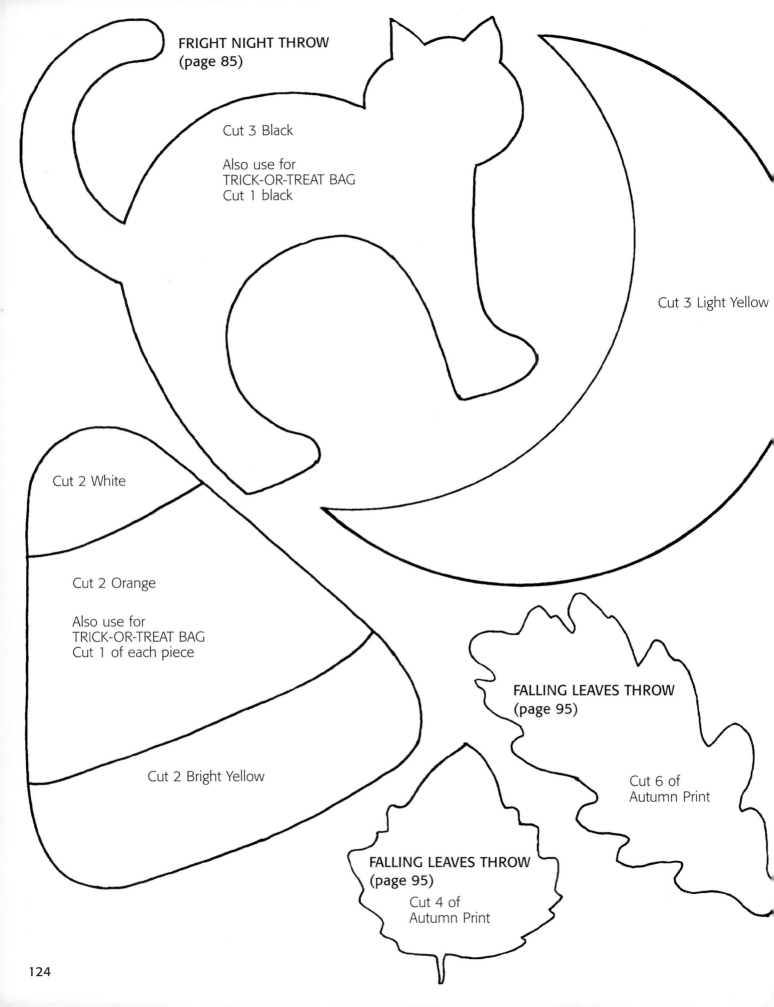

FRIGHT NIGHT THROW
(page 85)

Cut 3 Black

Also use for
TRICK-OR-TREAT BAG
Cut 1 black

Cut 3 Light Yellow

Cut 2 White

Cut 2 Orange

Also use for
TRICK-OR-TREAT BAG
Cut 1 of each piece

Cut 2 Bright Yellow

FALLING LEAVES THROW
(page 95)

Cut 6 of
Autumn Print

FALLING LEAVES THROW
(page 95)

Cut 4 of
Autumn Print

124

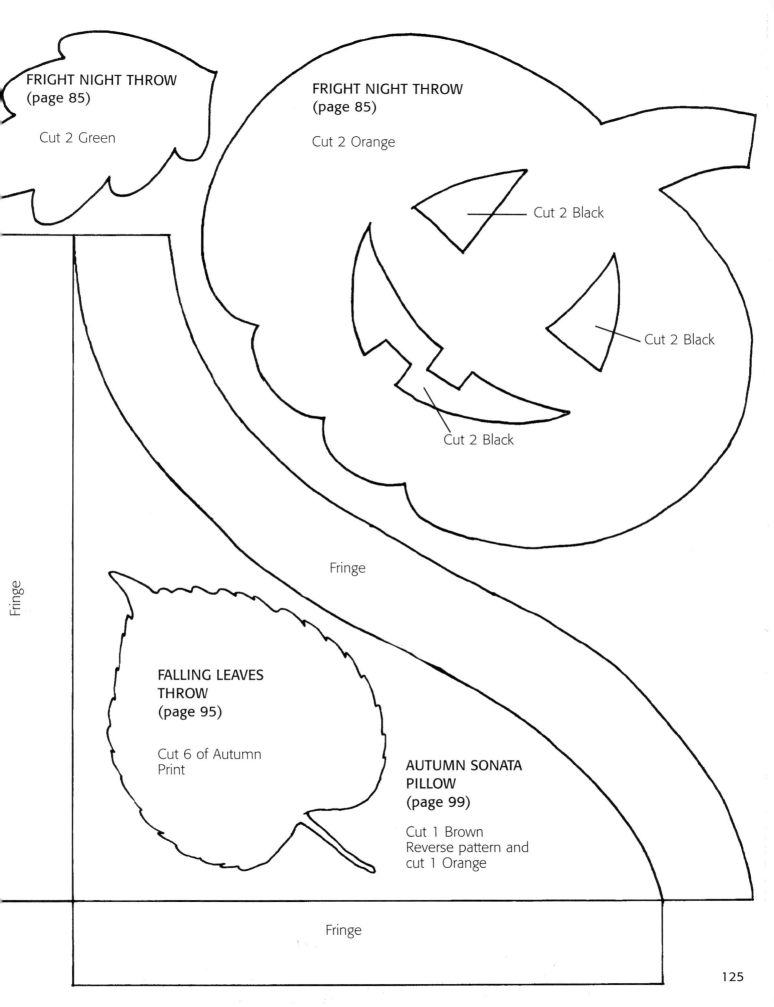

FRIGHT NIGHT THROW
(page 85)

Cut 2 Green

FRIGHT NIGHT THROW
(page 85)

Cut 2 Orange

Cut 2 Black

Cut 2 Black

Cut 2 Black

Fringe

Fringe

**FALLING LEAVES
THROW**
(page 95)

Cut 6 of Autumn
Print

**AUTUMN SONATA
PILLOW**
(page 99)

Cut 1 Brown
Reverse pattern and
cut 1 Orange

Fringe

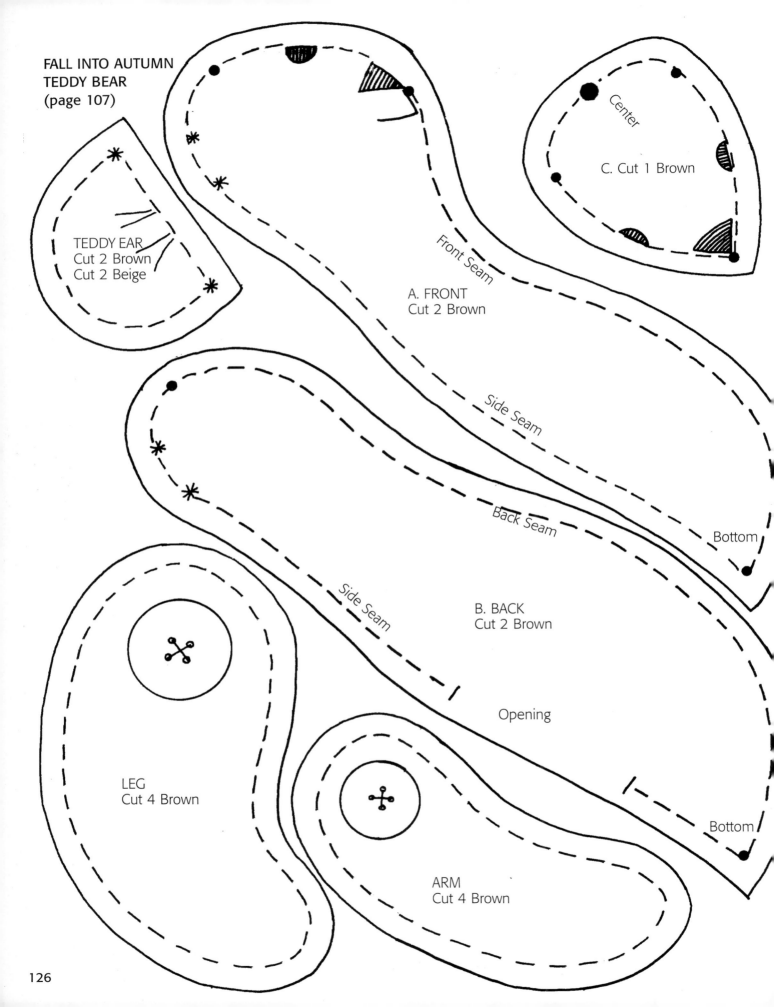

FALL INTO AUTUMN TEDDY BEAR
(page 107)

TEDDY EAR
Cut 2 Brown
Cut 2 Beige

Center

C. Cut 1 Brown

Front Seam

A. FRONT
Cut 2 Brown

Side Seam

Back Seam

Bottom

Side Seam

B. BACK
Cut 2 Brown

LEG
Cut 4 Brown

Opening

Bottom

ARM
Cut 4 Brown

126

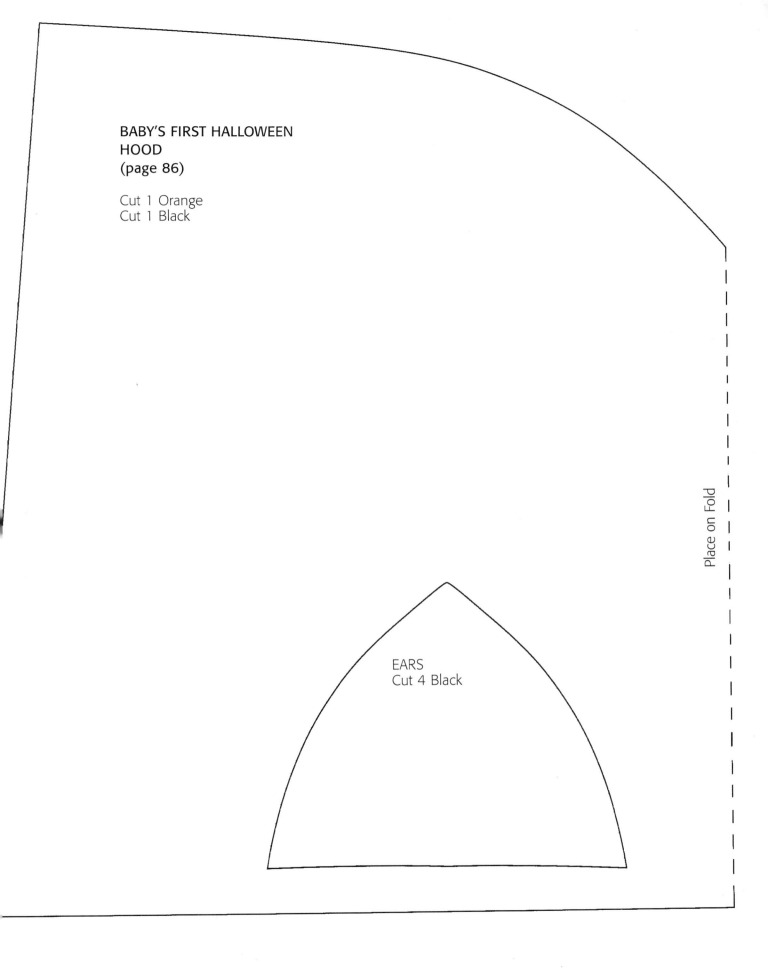

**BABY'S FIRST HALLOWEEN
HOOD**
(page 86)

Cut 1 Orange
Cut 1 Black

EARS
Cut 4 Black

Place on Fold

SOURCES & CREDITS

Most of the supplies used in this book can be found in your local fabric stores. If you can't find the item you're looking for, consult the following companies to find out where their products are sold:

Trims
Trimtex Company Inc. &
Carolace Industries
400 Park Avenue
Williamsport, PA 17701
570-326-9135
www.trimtex.com

Fusing Tapes and Fusible Web
Steam-A-Seam2®
The Warm Company
954 E. Union Street
Seattle, WA 98122

Chacopel Pencils
Clover
1007 E. Dominguez St.
Carson, CA 90746
(310) 516-7846

Foam Stamps
Plaid Enterprises
3225 Westech Dr.
Norcross, GA 30092
www.plaidonline.com

We'd like to thank Matthew Bower of Trimtex Company and Jacque Tupper of The Warm Company for their invaluable help with this book.

Special acknowledgement is given to our models Aubreanna Ochoa (pages 23, 44 & 79) and Brooke Ochoa(page 87). Also thanks to our canine model, Cassie (page 78).

Banar Designs Principals:
Barbara Finwall and Nancy Javier
Art Direction: Barbara Finwall
Editorial Direction: Nancy Javier
Photography: Stephen Whalen

Computer Graphic Design: Dana Allison
Project Direction: Jerilyn Clements
Designs by: Nancy Javier, Jerilyn Clements,
Barbara Finwall, Holly Witt Allen, and Dana Whalen

Published by

LEISURE ARTS
the art of everyday living
LEISURE ARTS
5701 Ranch Drive
Little Rock, AR 72223
© 2004 by Leisure Arts, Inc.

Produced by

BANAR DESIGNS
P.O. Box 483
Fallbrook, CA 92088
banar@adelphia.net

The information in this publication is presented in good faith, but no warranty is given, nor results guaranteed. Since we have no control over physical conditions surrounding the application of information herein contained, Leisure Arts, Inc. disclaims any liability for untoward results.